UNDER
THE BAR

UNDER THE BAR

THE BAR

TWELVE LESSONS OF LIFE FROM
THE WORLD OF POWERLIFTING

DAVETATE

Under the Bar

*Twelve Lessons of Life from the
World of Powerlifting*

Dave Tate

Copyright © 2005 Dave Tate

Published by:
Elite Fitness Systems
122 South Main Street
London, Ohio 43140

Printed in the United States of America.

Cover and layout: Ad Graphics, Inc., Tulsa, OK

ISBN: 978-0-9767838-0-0

Dedication

To
Blaine Michael Tate
Bryce David Tate

You are the best things that have
ever happened in my life.

Contents

Acknowledgments 9

Introduction 11

Chapter One: Aim 15

Chapter Two: Attitude 25

Chapter Three: Integrity 35

Chapter Four: Honesty 41

Chapter Five: Teamwork 47

Chapter Six: Criticism 59

Chapter Seven: Education 75

Chapter Eight: Risk Management 87

Chapter Nine: Perseverance 97

Chapter Ten: Flexibility 107

Chapter Eleven: Execution 117

Chapter Twelve: Responsibility 125

Summary: Loading the Bar 135

About Dave Tate 139

Acknowledgments

Special thanks to:

My parents: Thank you for the support and guidance throughout the years. Most important, for teaching me the values and skills needed to be successful as a leader, friend, husband, and father. I love you both.

Louie Simmons: Thank you for being a friend, mentor, and coach. Your example and dedication has had a profound effect on thousands of lifters across the world. I for one will be forever grateful.

The staff at Elitefts.com: Jim Wendler, Matt Bash, Lucy Burgees, Ken Hicks, and Traci Arnold-Tate. Thank you for helping my dreams come true. You guys have helped grow EliteFTS to a level I only dreamed about.

To the guys on our Q&A forum: I have not forgotten you. Thanks for keeping my mind open to new training methods. You are all making a difference in how the world gets stronger.

To all those who have inspired me to be my best: There are far too many of you to mention, but you all know who you are. Thanks for giving me your time and guidance.

And finally, to Traci Arnold-Tate, my partner and best friend: Thank you for always being there for me. Your support has been my driving force in more ways than I can count. I love you.

Introduction

I've been in the sport of powerlifting since I was 14 years old. In many ways you can say I've grown up in a weight room. I've had many ups and downs in the sport but would not change a thing. I will continue to stay a part of powerlifting for the rest of my life, and this book is one of many ways I've dedicated myself to giving back to the sport.

I wrote my first "Under the Bar" article in the summer of 2004 and did not know how it would go over. It was unlike any article I had written in the past. All my other articles had been designed to help the coach, trainer, and athlete improve their performance through superior strength and conditioning techniques. After many years of writing these types of articles I still felt something was missing, and that I had to find a better way to communicate these training techniques to my readers while connecting the concepts to every area of life in a holistic way.

For example, I could not understand how so many lifters and coaches could experience such great success in the weight room, yet the rest of their life was falling apart! They couldn't see that they already had all the skills they needed to be successful in all areas of their life, but they just could not make the connection. They knew how to set goals, work hard, and execute, but when it came to other areas of their life, they forgot the process. At the same time, many others suffered in their training because they did not see that those factors they used outside the weight room could make a difference *inside* the weight room.

These values were all introduced to me by my parents when I was a child. Most of our parents raised us with the values we would need to be successful. I was taught the difference between right and wrong; not to lie, steal or cheat; never to give up when things got hard; to value education; to have a positive attitude; to be flexible and keep my word; to work as part of a team and set my sights high. Many of you were also taught the same things. As a parent, I am now finding out that you can only teach so much. We can lay the groundwork, but it's up to our kids to make their own mistakes. While we all try our best to put our children on the right track, the fact is, they will never learn unless they find out for themselves through their own life experiences. The values we teach will always be their base of support, however, and the rules they've learned will help them play the game of life.

My parents did an outstanding job of raising me with high values, but as any other kid, I did not really learn the meaning of many of these things until life smacked me in the face. Fortunately for me, there were always people along the way to keep me on course. I now see that a child is not raised solely by their parents: A child is fully raised by all those he surrounds himself or herself with. What you'll find in this book are stories and principles that helped shape my life and make it what it is today.

Am I a success? I guess that depends on whom you speak to. Then again, does it? Yes, I feel I'm successful. I don't have millions of dollars, I don't hold any world powerlifting records, and I don't have a story of rising from the ashes. But I do live life on my own terms, I have a wonderful wife and family, great friends, a growing company, and most of all, I'm happy with what I've become.

I feel the success I've achieved was first learned in the home and then reinforced . . . under the bar.

The following chapters outline the fundamental values necessary for success in sports, in relationships—in life. They're best read in order, but if you're the type who can't follow orders, then you can dip into the book anywhere you like. Either way, stop to think about what each quality or principle means in your life and how you can strengthen the role it plays in achieving your goals.

Chapter One

Aim

· · · · ·

Success demands singleness of purpose.
Vince Lombardi

*Let him who would move the world
first move himself.*
Socrates

*A journey of a thousand miles
begins with a single step.*
Confucius

Have a vision not clouded by fear.
Cherokee proverb

*Where there is no vision,
the people perish.*
Proverbs 29:18

*The most important key to achieving great success
is to decide upon your goal and launch,
get started, take action, move.*

John Wooden

*If you do not stand for something,
you will fall for anything.*

Unknown

*Beliefs and convictions provide the boundaries
and direction that people want and need
in order to perform well.*

Don Shula

*Just because a man lacks use of his eyes
doesn't mean he lacks vision.*

Stevie Wonder

*Great things are not something accidental,
but must certainly be willed.*

Vincent Van Gogh

*Important principles
may and must be inflexible.*

Abraham Lincoln

Aim (as defined by the American Heritage Dictionary):
1. To direct toward or intend for a particular goal or group.
2. To determine a course or direct an effort.

Vision (as defined by the American Heritage Dictionary):
1. Unusual competence in discernment or perception; intelligent foresight.
2. The manner in which one sees or conceives something.
3. A mental image produced by the imagination.

Childhood Dreams

Everybody has a dream. They go way back to when you were a kid and wanted to be a fireman, policeman, cowboy, or a thousand other things. The only thing I can ever remember wanting to be was a powerlifter. Since the day I touched a weight, I loved it. Training was the best thing in life for me, and I loved the challenge of trying to become better. I can remember being asked time and time again what I was going to do with my life and really having no idea. I wanted to lift weights and that was it. The first time I read *Powerlifting USA* and saw how strong one can really be, I knew one day I would also lift the "big weights." The weights these guys were lifting were huge compared to what I was doing, and in many cases were more than twice my personal best. This didn't matter to me. I didn't know how I would do it or how long it would take, but I knew where I was and where I wanted to be. I figured all I had to do was fill in the blanks. Just turning 14, I had it all figured out. I knew the secret to success. It just took me another 20 years to figure out how much—or how little—I knew back then.

I had a vision of who I wanted to be and how it would feel to be that person. I would spend hours drawing barbells loaded with the "big weights" I would lift one day. In my vision I would be one of the best in my weight class. My vision was very clear: I figured I would be in the 275-weight class, even though I was only 181 at the time. I knew it would take 10 years or more. I knew I would have to do the work and become smarter about training. My vision set the path for me to achieve my goal.

I see the same intense vision in other lifters I've met along the way. I have seen lifters do amazing things, like squat more than 1,100 pounds, bench press 900 pounds, and deadlift more than 900 pounds. Without faith and vision, these lifts would have never been achievable.

The next section has been reinforced by principles I've learned in the development of elitefts.com. I've always known the principles, but it was through my business mentors that I learned how to communicate them in a very understandable way. The concepts of Primary Aim, Strategic Objective, and Key Strategic Indicators have been taken from *The E-Myth* by Michael Gerber.

Aim

I define "aim" as the main target you are shooting for and what you will do to get there. Many others may call this mission, conviction, or character. To me they are all the same and a very important part of your overall success strategy. I have worked with other coaches and lifters in the past and did not begin to incorporate aim into the strategy until a couple of years ago. Like many others, I would help lifters set up programs based on what they told me and then set them free. While this seemed to work and gave them what they needed, I always knew there had to be more if the program was to be successful in the long run. I knew the formula from my own past experience and for the first time am sharing it with the public. Pay attention here. This information is huge and has also had a huge impact on the way Elitefts.com does business.

First, you need to establish what your main aim is. Who do you want to be? What do you want to be remembered for? This is not just for training—it's for everything. If you were to fast-forward to the young age of 85, as you sit in your rocking chair, what do you want to be able to look back on? If your grand-children were to ask, "What did you do with your life?"—what would you like to say? If you are a lifter and they were to ask, "How much did you deadlift?"—what do you want to say? Let's go further ahead and say you have passed this world and moved on to the next. How would you like your eulogy to read? What will your headstone say? What will people say at your funeral? How will your friends remember you? Family? Coworkers? Acquaintances? How do you want to leave this world?

The Prize

I know these are all pretty deep questions, but we need to think about them from time to time and consider whether we're doing what we really want to be doing. We only go around the world one time and should all strive to make the best of it. If you've been to very many sporting events, you sometimes see half-time shows where a spectator is called to the floor by seat number or raffle ticket and asked to do a specific task. If they complete the task, they win a prize. They may be asked to toss a ball through a hoop, kick a field goal, or a number of other things. Many times they're given only one shot at the task, and if they don't make it, they go back to their seat without the prize. If they do complete the task, they go back with more than they walked to the floor with—and also gave the audience something to remember. When the contestants are called to the line to toss the ball (or whatever the task), do you think they're going to half-ass the attempt or give it everything they've got? Of course, they'll try their hardest—there's a prize on the line. Now let me ask you a few more questions: What is a bigger prize, a trip to Disney World or your life? Why would you go through life not giving it your all?

The Gap

The important thing to remember is the gap. The gap is where we're all at right now. The gap is what we have control of. If you thought about the earlier questions, then you know how you would like to be remembered and what type of impact you would like to make. You also know who you have become up until this time. Has your past dictated the future you would like to have? If you died today, how will you be remembered? If you don't like the way you'd be remembered if you left us today, then you still have the gap. The gap is the space between where you are and how you will be remembered. None of us knows how big or small this gap may be, so there is no time to mess around. When you decide how you would like to be, then get right to work and be it! There is no tomorrow, next week, or next year. There is only now. When you begin to fill the gap with how you want to be, you'll quickly find that's who you are. After you decide on how you would like to live your life, create a statement for it. Take your time with this. This will become your primary aim. To give you an example, I use: "to live, learn, and pass on." This idea has a very important meaning for me, one that I keep to myself, the same way you will keep yours to yourself. You may even set up different aims for different aspects of your life. For those I help with training programs, we set one up just for their training, but only after a main aim has been developed. The main aim will be a source for all the principles and values you'll keep throughout your life.

Objective

Now that your main aim has been developed, we can move on to the next step. What is your objective for the next five years? We will use a powerlifting program as an example to illustrate the point of this process. We will assume the lifter has developed his training aim and set it up as "To be one of the best amateur lifters and coaches on the West Coast." Lifter A has a very nonspecific aim. This is good because it makes it flexible and inflexible at the same time. Based on this aim, we can see the word "amateur." This implies to the lifter that he will not use any strength-training drugs such as steroids. In the sport of powerlifting, "amateur" and "drug-free" mean the same thing. We also see that, for this aim to be accomplished, we will need to fill in the gap. This is done with a written objective. This objective should be no longer than one page and should list the details of what will need to be done in the next five years to live up to this objective. The meat of the objectives should include:

1. What weight classes will he lift in?
2. How many meets per year will be the average?
3. What will the main powerlifts need to be to become one of the best lifters on the West Coast?
4. How much will he need to lift in his main supplemental lifts to achieve the main powerlift goals?
5. How much weight will he need to use in his max-effort training lifts to achieve his main powerlifting goals?

6. How much weight will he have to be using in the accessory lifts to achieve his main lift, max effort, and supplemental lift goals?

7. How many athletes will he be training at the end of the five years?

8. What type of athletes will they be?

9. What will their lifts be?

Many other topics remain to be discussed in the objective. The key is to list all the things that will need to happen for the aim to be achievable. The aim is not a static thing: It keeps moving, so you don't want to think that all you need is five years to achieve your aim. Remember: Your aim is not a goal—it's a vision of who you want to be. Your goals will come later. We use five years because one year is too short and more than five is too long. Five years is a great time frame to make huge changes.

Indicators

After you've written your objective, go back through and look for all the specific indicators you can find. Our powerlifter would look for items such as:

1. My squat will be 700 pounds.

2. My floor press will have to be 465 pounds if I want to bench press 525.

3. I will obtain my elite total in the 242-pound weight class.

4. By the end of five years, I will be training 20 high school football players.

The list would continue until every indicator is found. These will become your key strategic indicators to help you track if you're on the right path. If you keep a written record of each of these indicators and review them at the end of each month or each training cycle, then you'll always know exactly where you are, whether you're going forward or backward, and exactly what indicators are off. When you know what indicators are off, then it's easy to get back on track, because you don't have to fix everything—you only have to fix the part that's broken. If you needed new tires for a car, would you go out and buy a new car? This is exactly what many lifters do with their training programs; if one aspect is not working, they kill the entire process and begin with a complete new program that they have no experience with. All they have to do is fix the one aspect that is not working and they're back on track. This process helps keep you on track. The more indicators you have, the better. We have more than 70 specific indicators that are tracked on a daily, weekly, and monthly basis at Elitefts.com. This one process has been the biggest driving force behind the growth and success of the company, and it was all learned in a nonspecific way . . . "under the bar."

One More Thing

I still remember the vision I had when I was 14. I didn't care what I did for a living as long as I could always be around people lifting big weights. I guess you could say this was my childhood dream. Today, when I realize that I'm actually living my dream and remember all those who told me it could not be done, I wonder why so many sell out on their dreams. If I could make my dreams come true, then they can, too—and so can you. What is your aim in life?

Chapter Two

Attitude

*Human beings, by changing the inner
attitudes of their minds, can change the
outer aspects of their lives.*

William James

*Weakness of attitude becomes
weakness of character.*

Albert Einstein

*Ability is what you're capable of doing.
Motivation determines what you do.
Attitude determines how well you do it.*

Lou Holtz

*Attitude is a little thing that
makes a big difference.*

Winston Churchill

*Our attitude toward others determines
their attitude towards us.*

Earl Nightingale

*Great effort springs naturally
from a great attitude.*

Pat Riley

*I discovered I always have choices and
sometimes it's only a choice of attitude.*

Judith M. Knowlton

*Motivation determines what you do.
Attitude determines how well you do it.*

Raymond Chandler

*Nothing can stop the man with the right
mental attitude from achieving his goal;
nothing on earth can help the man
with the wrong mental attitude.*

Thomas Jefferson

Attitude (as defined by the American Heritage Dictionary):

1. A position of the body or manner of carrying oneself.
2. A state of mind or a feeling; disposition.
3. A relatively stable and enduring predisposition to behave or react in a characteristic way.
4. A complex mental state involving beliefs and feelings and values and dispositions to act in certain ways.

Your Choice

At EFS we define attitude as approaching life and work with passion, a smile, and a positive state of mind. We strongly believe our attitude determines our success in the marketplace. I selected this as a company value for several reasons, but the most important is that I have seen how attitude has made a difference in my own (and others') training over the years. Attitude is a key ingredient to success "under the bar" as well as in business and life.

Some may feel attitude is all about positive thinking and motivation. While this is true to some degree, motivation and positive thinking are both temporary, while attitude should be a part of who you are. Attitude is a clear indication of who you really are and who you really want to be. If you are not where you'd like to be—or at least on your way—then the first place to look is attitude. The most important thing to keep in mind is that YOU choose your attitude in response to any give situation. Regardless of what someone has done to you, you choose how to react to it. Let me explain with a few "under the bar" examples.

Chuck Vogelpoh

Chuck Vogelpohl has become known for his unbelievable training and competitive spirit. In his recent training video *Westside Secrets Chuck Vogelpohl XXX,* you can see a great example of his training and competitive attitude. In one of his squatting sessions, Chuck begins to work up in weight to get a better feel of the heavier weight and his equipment. After a few sets of increased weight, Chuck is now close to his max. On this particular set, Chuck unracked the weight and began his descent to the box. He did not finish the weight and ended up having the spotters pull the weight back to the racks. Most lifters I know would have called it a day and been happy with a "nice try." Not Chuck. He had a different attitude about the situation and called for one more try—but this time asked for the spotters to add *another 50 pounds* to the bar. On his next set Chuck not only squatted the weight but also did it for two reps.

JL Holdsworth

You may all know JL Holdsworth for his contribution to the elitefts.com Q&A forum, but a few of us from Westside know him for more than his training advice. I knew from the first training session JL took at Westside that he had the right attitude to succeed in the sport of powerlifting. A great example of JL's attitude was seen at the 2004 APF Senior Nationals. JL's training for the meet went very well, and we knew there would be big things in store for him. JL started off the day with an easy squat opener and then jumped to a 900 pounds for a new PR (personal record). JL had missed this weight at his last two competitions and was looking forward to another shot at it. On his second attempt JL missed the weight, and the spotters had to help him back to the rack. JL repeated the weight for his third attempt. This would be the fifth time he has tried this weight, with four misses already. JL set up the squat and made it look very easy as he stood up and racked the weight for a good lift. JL then opened his bench with an easy 733 and then jumped to 777 for his second. He pressed the weight to the top with very little problem but was red-lighted a bad lift for his hips coming up. JL repeated the weight and missed it again for the same reason. JL could have been very upset with this, as he had the same problem a couple of months before, when he attempted 800 pounds. He was really looking forward to an 800-pound bench press. With the deadlift coming up, JL found that he was in a very tight race with two other lifters, both of whom also have great attitudes. We did not know how JL would end up, as his best pull was 760 pounds, while we knew he would need all of that plus more to win this class. JL ended up pulling 805 for a personal record and the win. JL willed himself to pull what he needed to put himself on top. JL had a great day and should be proud of what he accomplished, but all he can think of now is getting ready for the next meet, where the stakes and lifts will be higher.

Jeff "Gritter" Adams

Jeff Adams, like myself, spent many years and many attempts trying to bench press 600 pounds. I am not exactly sure how many times he had missed this weight but I do know it was more than I had. I missed the weight more than 10 times before finally making it a couple of years ago. Jeff has a very extensive injury history and has spent more time being beat up than almost any lifter I have ever known over the years. Jeff's great attitude, however, kept him hard at work trying to reach his goal of 600 pounds. Regardless of how and why he missed the weight, he would always go back to the drawing board and come up with a new plan of attack without ever letting the last miss hold him back. After many years he finally found the right plan of attack, and at the 2003 Outlaws bench/deadlift meet Jeff finally made the weight. I was there for this lift and have to say it was one of the more memorable lifts I've ever seen. This lift was not memorable because it was 600 pounds: It was memorable because it was a great display of an attitude that had overcome much adversity to reach a goal. Success!

How to Keep a Great Attitude

I could keep listing examples like this dating back to the first day I walked into a "real" gym and was approached by a few powerlifters who offered to help me out. It's not very often you find men in their 30s offering to take the time to help a 14-year-old kid with his training. Throughout the years I have seen many great examples of positive attitudes that have all led to great success. I have also seen many examples of very poor attitudes that have always lead to sub par results and unhappiness. And it's guaranteed that those with poor attitudes will always try to bring you down to their level. This is one way they have found to make themselves feel better. You can see this negative behavior all over the Internet now, and spreading every day. Nevertheless, I've learned a few basic concepts over the years that have helped me keep a great attitude. These concepts have helped shape my training, business and life. These include:

Share Time with Great People

Keep company with those people who have the same attitude you would like to have. Being at Westside has made a huge, positive difference in my training. The staff at EFS has also had a huge impact on the growth and success of the company; without them it would still be an "at home" operation being run out of my spare bedroom. Family has also been as positive force and will continue to be—when you do what I do (powerlifting and running a business), family is the only balance you have. My family could care less about how many lifts I make or how business is going. What they really care about is how *I'm* doing. I learned a couple of years ago, with the birth of my first son, that family is what keeps us all in balance and complete.

Let It Go

When things go wrong, as they inevitably will, then learn from the mistakes—and let it go. OK, so I may still need some work on this one, but I've learned "under the bar" that a missed lift is not the end of the world and doesn't mean you will *always* miss the weight. What it means is you need to find out why it happened, learn from it—then let it go. This is also true with your personal life and business; it's just much harder to do in "real life" than in the weight room. There are many times where something is said that will fire me up, and while I know I should let it go, I have a hard time doing it. My solution is to try and keep these incidents behind closed doors, with those who know I'm just blowing off steam and may even take it upon themselves to bring me back to reality. Yet even with close friends and associates, I always have to remember what I'm upset about and to whom I'm speaking. For example, I may be pissed because our sales are down, and that means we may be in the red for the month. I can't bitch about it to my staff: If something's wrong with the business, it's not their fault—it's mine! This is the responsibility I took up when the company was founded. At the same time, if things are going very well and we're having a great month, then it's never due to something I did—it's due to what they did! In other words, you have to be very selective about what you say and to whom you say it.

Decide How It Will Be

Decide what type of day you'll have: When you wake up, you need to decide right then and there that it will be a great, productive day that will help lead you to your goals. This is truer than you think. Who really decides how you'll feel? Only you can talk yourself into a bad day. Yes, bad things can happen, but when they do, you need to realize that the number of days we have on this earth are limited and this one bad thing is not worth the cost of one precious day of your life.

Execution

Being positive is not enough. Let's face it, you can resolve to think 100% positive thoughts and never let anything bother you, but this is just not going to happen. Even if it did, it will not *produce* anything without action and execution. You have to be able to pick the right things to do and then execute them effectively. Execution will be discussed in a future *Under the Bar* chapter. Let's face it: If you say you want to bench press 500 pounds but don't train for it, the odds of it happening are slim. You need to find the best plan you can and get to work on it, and try to do something each day to help you achieve your goal.

The Effect on Others

Your attitude will determine the attitude of those around you. Have you ever noticed that when you're in a good mood, everyone else seems to be in a good mood? Have you also noticed that when you're in a bad mood, everyone else is also upset? This can be seen in any gym or team environment. The next time you go to the gym to train with your team or training partner, go in with a fired-up, positive attitude, and you'll notice that the rest of the crew will also be fired up. This is a great reason to have a number of training partners and one reason why Westside is so great. If you feel like crap and don't have the right attitude, more than likely someone else will have a great attitude and it will rub off on you. This is the same approach I used when selecting the current staff at EFS. I was looking for different types of personalities that would fit together and help keep the wheels moving, even when someone may be having an "off" day.

Purpose

No matter what happens, it has its purpose. This is a tough one, and I think the most important on this list. This is about suffering a great loss or a huge injury, going bankrupt, or enduring some other tragedy or trauma. It may not even be of that magnitude, but it's huge to you and words can't define it, which is why it may be hard for anyone else to understand the significance of the event. The point is, it changes your life. How it changes your life may not be seen for years to come, but sooner or later you will begin to see a pattern of events that leads to something—believe it or not—that turns out to be very good for you. A personal example: The day I tore my pec off was one of the worst days of my life. I felt that I was done with powerlifting, as my surgeon told me. But when I look back, it was one of the best things that has ever happened to me. This event is one of the main reasons I decided to move to Columbus. This then led to a series of events—training at Westside, working as personal trainer, founding EFS—that has changed my life in more ways than just training. There have been many other major events that have changed my life that seemed very bad at first but led the way to bigger and better things. The key is to try and remember this while you're suffering through the bad parts.

We Are Not Perfect

I could write an entire book about attitude. While nobody can be expected to have the best attitude 100% of the time, it is more important to try to do better in this area. We'll all have our bad days, say things without thinking, and think there are many things we just can't do—this is normal. We can, however, always work on keeping a positive outlook and try to help others do the same. Always keep in mind how you'd like to be remembered when you leave this world. I know how I'd like to be remembered and work hard at achieving that goal each day. Do you?

Chapter Three

Integrity

*It is not the oath that makes us believe the man,
but the man the oath.*

Aeschylus

*Faced with crisis, the man of character
falls back upon himself.*

Charles De Gaulle

*Whoever is careless with the truth
in small matters cannot be trusted
with the important matters.*

Albert Einstein

*The ultimate measure of a man is not
where he stands in moments of comfort
and convenience, but where he stands
at times of challenge.*

The Rev. Martin Luther King Jr.

If you do not stand for something,
you will stand for anything.

Ginger Rogers

Worry not that no one knows of you;
seek to be worth knowing.

Confucius

He who plants thorns must never
expect to gather roses.

English proverb

Never worry about number.
Help one person at a time,
and always start with the person nearest you.

Mother Teresa

Integrity (as defined by the American Heritage Dictionary):

1. Steadfast adherence to a strict moral or ethical code.

2. The state of being unimpaired; soundness.

3. The quality or condition of being whole or undivided; completeness.

What Behavior Do You Behave In?

Brian Tracy defined integrity as a value that guarantees all other values and the quality that locks in your values and causes you to live consistent with them. Integrity is the highest value and the one that will set the stage for how you approach your personal relationships, training, and business—how you will live your life. If you're an honest person, then you should be an honest person all the time, not when it's convenient. If you want to know what type of person you are, you need to look at what types of behavior you engage in and what values you deem the most important to you.

Everything I needed to know I learned "under the bar." I've always tried to surround myself with the best lifters of the highest level of integrity, and have been fortunate to learn from their examples.

Louie Simmons

A great example of high integrity is high-quality training. Louie Simmons is a great example of this. Louie is always in the gym early, stays late, and concentrates on every detail needed to advance his training and the training of lifters around the world. He lives this value 24 hours a day and has been known to train up to 17 sessions per week. I've never seen him turn a lifter away, and he'll spend hours on the phone each day helping lifters and coaches work through their problems. An example that comes immediately to mind occurred one afternoon when I met Louie at his home. I forget now where we had to go but do remember it was a very important meeting. Louie was on the phone with a novice lifter when I walked in. It was very apparent that the lifter on the other end didn't have a clue about how we trained. The answers I overheard Louie give were very basic and have been covered many times in the articles he has written for Power Lifting USA. Louie took his time and answered every question asked. Meanwhile, I realized we had to get out of there ASAP or we were going to be late for our meeting. To put it kindly, I was *stressing* about this. I hate to be late for anything! Yet Louie didn't show any signs of stress and kept helping this lifter out. By the time he got off the phone, our appointment time had already passed. Louie didn't say a word as we finally left for the meeting. Yes, we were late, but I learned something about Louie that day that I will never forget: Helping others should always come before helping yourself. This made a huge impact on me and should serve as a constant reminder to us all.

Do the Right Thing

Who you are inside will always be shown by the actions you take every day. This is especially true when you're forced to make an important decision. Having integrity means doing what you believe to be the right thing every time, even if it doesn't result in the best outcome at the beginning. At EFS, we strive to offer the highest level of customer service and have a great track record for this. We still make mistakes, as we all do. The difference is that we'll go out of our way to make these mistakes right. I've been advised by many people I respect that there are times when you should "fire" the client or customer just to get rid of them. This has always made me uncomfortable and is one thing I've always disagreed with. What if that person was me?

What if It Was Me?

Because of our commitment to integrity—and the customer— at Elitefts.com, there have been times when we not only lost our total profit margin on a deal but also ran deep in the hole. We'll never back away from ensuring that the customer is satisfied with our performance, even if we lose money on the deal. Yet I've been told that this is a mistake, because the odds of them ever ordering from us again drop by 80%, so all we're doing is throwing money away. While this may be the case, we still have to ask, "What if it was me?"

Integrity Development

So how do you develop a high level of integrity? The first thing I would suggest is to determine what values you hold in the highest regard. If you don't know what these are, then examine the people you hold in high regard. Why do you admire them? When you think about why you admire these people, you'll discover what values are the most important to you. Now ask yourself if you live your life by these same values. If so, do you live by them in *every* situation? Are you consistent with your values? Do you keep your word?

A second way to determine what values you have is to ask those around you what they believe you stand for. Make sure to ask people who are friends, family, and even those who may not like you at all. Get as much feedback as you can. Is this feedback how you want to be remembered? If it isn't, then you can change—but only if you want to. Life is too short not to be remembered the way you want. Do you want to be remembered as the guy who screwed everyone for a buck, treated his wife like crap, spent little time with his kids, had no friends, and did nothing to make the world a better place? Or would you like to be remembered as a great coach, husband, father, and friend who helped make a positive difference in the world? Living a life of integrity is the first and best way to leave a legacy to be proud of.

Chapter Four

Honesty

*The best measure of a man's honesty
isn't his income tax return.
It's the zero adjust on his bathroom scale.*

Arthur C. Clarke

*Honesty pays, but it doesn't seem to pay
enough to suit some people.*

F. M. Hubbar

*Where is there dignity
unless there is honesty?*

Cicero

No legacy is so rich as honesty.

William Shakespeare

Honesty is a question of right or wrong,
not a matter of policy.

Author unknown

Honesty is the first chapter
in the book of wisdom.

Thomas Jefferson

Each time you are honest and conduct
yourself with honesty, a success force
will drive you toward greater success.
Each time you lie, even with a little white lie,
there are strong forces pushing
you toward failure.

Joseph Sugarman

Honesty (as defined by the American Heritage Dictionary):

1. The quality or condition of being honest; integrity.
2. Truthfulness; sincerity: *in all honesty.*

The Promise

One of the biggest promises I have ever made in my life was made to a woman I knew for only a few days and will probably never see again. Yet, that promise had a major impact on many lives and will continue to for many years to come. (I'll explain in more detail at the end of this chapter.)

Win/Lose Relationships

Many times people will give you their word only to break it the next day. The worst part of this is that it can become such a common event that, when you find someone who is honest and keeps his or her word, it is seen as a rarity. Being dishonest has even become a glorified process that can be seen just about every night on TV. What message is this really sending? "Hey, it's no big deal if you're dishonest and lie, as long as you get what you want!" This will only create a temporary win, because you are in a win/lose situation. In this case, you win in the short term while the other party loses. This is great for the winner for now, but in the long run, you can count on never gaining the trust and respect of the other party, and thus kill any future relationship you could have had. This win is not worth the future loss to your reputation.

Lose/Win Relationships

The next option is to give in to every need and demand of the other party, creating a lose/win situation. While this is great for the second party, it will create more stress for you than you need or deserve. We've all found ourselves in this position, and many of us are still living each day in compromised positions that we brought on ourselves. While the other party does not give it a second thought, you live each day thinking, "I should have said . . ." or "If I could do it again I would . . ." Well, you know something? You can always go back and make things right. You just have to have the courage to stand up for what you think is right. Most of us do not do this because it's easier to live with the pain of the poor decision than it is to create another, better situation. You really need to ask yourself if this is wise. If you take a chance by trying to find a better balance in your relationship, the confrontation you think will take place probably won't, and both you and the second party will walk away with a healthier relationship.

Win/Win Relationships

The last situation is win/win and is the best option for everyone. So why are there so few win/win solutions out there? To create a win/win solution requires work, communication, and the respect of both parties. There are many people out there who would rather just "give in" than state what they really feel. This is because they are scared of what the other party "might say or do." The truly interesting thing here is that many would rather deal with the pain of being taken advantage of than the pain of finding a win/win solution. Do not give in when you feel you are being taken advantage of. When you feel there is no other solution, then you're not looking hard enough. Granted, there are many people out there who would rather bully, upper hand, underhand, screw (or whatever you call it) anyone to get what they want. The biggest problem here is that if they get what they want (which is very unlikely), there will be nobody there to share it with, *plus* they will always feel like there is someone trying to take away what they have. The world has much to offer to everyone, and there will always be the greatest rewards for those who create the most win/win relationships throughout their lives. These win/win relations begin with keeping your word, doing what you say you will do, and treating everyone as you would like to be treated.

Deal with the Truth

What does all this have to do with keeping your word? It has everything to do with it. You have to know the nature of the relationship before you open your mouth and say something you will regret later. You need to take time and think before you speak. In today's world, a person's word means nothing. This is a very sad, yet true, thing. You really can't trust what anyone tells you and need always to look out for your own best interests. However, there are still people out there who choose to keep their word no matter what the outcome. I feel a man is only as good as his word, and that is the way it should be. Honesty broken once will be broken forever. A lie is a lie, and it doesn't matter if it's a white lie or a huge monster lie. Either way, in my book, you're a scumbag. Now just because I said you can't trust anyone does not mean you have to be like everyone else. As the old saying goes, "If everyone jumped off a bridge, would you?" You can be one of the few who are known as a trusted friend, business partner, parent, and spouse. This is not without its consequences. You have to be willing to deal with the truth. For many, it is much easier to lie than deal with the truth. The truth can be hard but can also free you. A lie is also hard, and you remain stuck with it. Nothing good can ever come of it. Look, I know many of you are thinking, "You don't know my wife, you don't know my boss—you don't know my

life." Correct: I don't know you and I'm not telling you to con-
fess everything you do. If you get to work late, you don't have to
run up and tell your boss you were late—but it's another thing
to mark your time card as if you were there on time. There is a
difference between not saying anything and telling a lie. That's
why we were all told as kids to keep our mouth shut until asked
to speak.

Take Care of Him

"Take care of him." With tears in her eyes, this was what was
asked of me by Blaine's birth mother as we departed with my
new son. Blaine was my first adopted son and one of the best
experiences of my life. I gave her my word that I would take
care of him, and I have no intention of breaking it. If I keep my
word, by the time Blaine reads this he will know the true meaning of "a promise." If I do not keep this promise, then he will
know I am not a man of my word. If you are a man or woman
of your word, then you will never have to tell anyone—they
will already know. What do they know about you?

The wealthiest man in the world
may not loan you money to make a phone call,
while the person who is very down on his luck
may just give you the world.

. . . .
DT

Chapter Five

Teamwork

. . . .

Individual commitment to a group effort—
that is what makes a team work, a company work,
a society work, a civilization work.

Vince Lombardi

A small group of thoughtful people could change
the world; indeed, it's the only thing that ever has.

Margaret Mead

A leader should not get too far in front
of his troops or he will be shot in the ass.

Joseph Clark

Great men are rarely isolated mountain peaks;
they are summits of ranges.

Thomas Wentworth Higginson

It is amazing what you can accomplish
if you do not care who gets the credit.

Harry Truman

Talent wins games, but teamwork and
intelligence win championships.

Michael Jordan

The only place success comes before
teamwork is in the dictionary.

Vince Lombardi

Teamwork is the ability to
work together toward a common vision.
The ability to direct individual accomplishments
toward organizational objectives.
It is the fuel that allows common people
to attain uncommon results.

Andrew Carnegie

Teamwork (as defined by the American Heritage Dictionary):

1. Cooperative effort by the members of a group or team to achieve a common goal.

Weakest Link

You are only as strong as your weakest link. How many times have we all read this? Have you ever really thought about it, or do you just read the words? What is your weakest link? Are you in the process of making this a stronger link? Are there others helping you with this? Could there be others who could help? What are your plans of attack? Could you be the weakest link of your team? Are you part of a team? Are you helping others strengthen their weakest link? These are all questions we should be asking ourselves each day.

The sport of powerlifting is all about getting a bigger total. Adding your best squat, bench press, and deadlift makes up this total. This is a very simple concept, but it can be very difficult to increase the strength of your best squat, bench press, or deadlift, especially all at the same time. Many lifters find that one or two of the three lifts will be moving for them very well, but there's always that one lift that becomes very hard to increase. This one lift becomes your weakest link and a great example of how relationships can have a positive effect on your training, business, and life.

Weak Triceps

We will assume your weakest link is the bench press. There are several factors needed to get your bench press moving. These include: strong lats, triceps, shoulders, and pecs, and a great lockout, bench press technique, and equipment. If your goal is to bench press 400 pounds and you have a 400-pound technique, 400-pound shoulders, 400-pound lats, 400-pound equipment, and 350-pound triceps, then you will have a 350-pound bench press. The triceps are your weakest link. When they are developed to match the other variables, you will have a 400-pound bench press. There is a relationship between the key factors that have to be given notice. All the above factors play a role in the success of the bench press, with the most important always being the weakest link.

The Others

So what does this have to do with relationships? Teamwork? Relationships and teamwork are one in the same. The example of weak triceps holding back the entire bench press shows how different relationships can have a profound effect on the final outcome. For true success, this principle extends far further than weak triceps and their role in the bench press. Like it or not, you are always part of a team. The individual is the most important aspect of the team, and many individuals have accomplished many great things, but there are always others who have helped along the way. These "others" are perhaps the most important components on your road to success in whatever you do.

Reverend Tony

Reverend Tony Hutson told the best story I ever heard about the importance of the relationships in life, during the wedding of Jim Wendler. Jim is the senior editor for ElitFTS. com and is an accomplished powerlifter. Jim was looking for something different for his wedding and asked Rev. Tony if he would preside over the service. Jim and Tony knew each other from lifting in many of the same powerlifting competitions, and Jim also knew Tony to be a great man with the highest morals. Rev. Tony is a Baptist minister from the Deep South—Tennessee. I have heard stories of how Tony would scream, yell, slobber, spit, and lose up to 15 pounds during a single sermon. His passion and willingness to travel six hours for a ceremony, then turn right around and drive back for church the next day is a testament to his great service to God and his willingness to help others. Tony is also a very accomplished powerlifter, with a 1,025-pound squat and 700-pound bench press to his name.

The wedding was an outdoors affair made up of family and close friends. All eyes were on Tony as he walked down the aisle scattered with rose pedals toward the place Jim and Whitney would say their vows. I still wonder what was going through the minds of the attendants as Tony made his entrance. It's not every day you see a 6'3" man weighing every bit of 385 walking across the lawn with a suit and tie. And Tony is not your typical 385-pound man; Tony is huge with a low body-fat percentage. Needless to say, he had everyone's attention.

The Squat

Half way trough the ceremony Tony began to speak about Jim being an accomplished powerlifter with a 940-pound squat. I began to wonder where Tony was going with this because only about four people in attendance knew what the sport of powerlifting was, let alone what a squat was. I, of course, knew, so he had my attention at least. He went on to say that, during the squat competition, the lifter is attempting to do something they have never done before. In Jim's case this would mean having more than 900 pounds on his back. While he has trained for this and should be ready, it is still a personal record and a weight he has never squatted before. In competition we would never think of squatting a record, or any weight for that matter, without spotters. During the squat there are spotters on both sides and in back of the lifter to make sure they can take the weight in case something goes wrong. If the lifter misses the weight, and the spotters are either not there or not paying attention, he will have to dump the bar, and both the lifter and bar will fall to the ground.

The Spotters

Tony went on to say that squatting is the same as life. Each of us needs to have spotters on each side and behind us. On the one side, you will have your true friends. These are your friends who've been with you through the good times and bad; they do not judge you for who you are or what you do. These friends appreciate you for who you are, not what you can do for them or what status you hold in society. These friends will always be there for you, whether it's lunch time or 4 a.m., without question. They are not friends who disappear when you need help but come back around when you have success. The spotters to the other side are your family. The family unit is one of the strongest units we as humans have. Your family will, and always should, love you unconditionally. The support you receive from your spouse and children can make the difference between success and failure. Your own parents and siblings will always know you for who you are and care what happens to you. Tony finished by stating that your back spotter is GOD. He will always be behind you, regardless of the situation. When you have strong spotters (family, faith, and friends), you can accomplish anything. If and when the weight gets too heavy, they will be there to catch it before you have to dump the bar. If the weight is still too heavy and you have to dump the bar, they will be there to help you get back up.

Expanded Relationships

While family, faith, and friends are the most important relationships you will have that make up your winning team, there are other relationships that can make all the difference in your success. These relationships include your acquaintances, the network you build, mentors, coworkers, team members, and yourself.

Acquaintances

It's important to look at whom you spend your time with. Do they share the same goals and values you do? You will become whomever you spend the most time with. As a child I always used to wonder why my parents were always so interested in who my friends were, where they lived, and who their parents were. This drove me out of my mind. Why did it matter where they lived or what their parents did? I knew kids with wealthy parents who lived in the best part of town, and these kids were into all kinds of drugs and always in trouble. I also knew kids from poor families who did their best to get by. These were great kids who may not have been the best students but were never in trouble. I knew these kids because they were many of my friends. We shared the same classes and played on the same sports teams. I later found out that my parents' interest was not really in what my friends' parents did for a living or where they lived, but it was just to check to see who they were so they could ask around about them. It did not take until later in life that I realized these kids were still my friends and my parents never said a thing to me about them. This was because they did check into them and agreed with the values these kids were raised with. Where someone is from and what he or she does is never an indication of who he or she really is or will be. If you spend your time with those who have nothing better to do than gossip about others, wish they had more, or complain about bad luck, then you, too, will also be wishing for more instead of making more for yourself. Do not let others hold you back.

Your Network

One of the biggest keys to relationship success is who can build the best network. What is a network? A network is a contact group of people who can help each other achieve their goals. I learned many years ago that before I could be successful "under the bar" I was going to have to know people who knew more than I did in many fields. I also knew I had something to bring to the table with the training knowledge I had developed throughout the years. I began to find a way to introduce myself to as many lifters, coaches, trainers, professors, and authors as I could. I then had a network of people whom I could toss ideas around with and come up with some great training ideas and plans that none of us alone could come up with. The biggest secret I have learned about networking throughout the years is that EVERYONE knows more about SOMETHING than you do. I highly suggest purchasing a contact-management program and begin putting everyone you know in it. You would be surprised how much of a difference this can make to your life.

Mentors

I feel many of us make our goals much harder to achieve than they should be because we don't seek out those who've already achieved what we want and ask them for help. I am always surprised that, whenever I contact people for help and advice, many of them are willing to help out. As a matter of fact, I have never been denied in this regard. I have found that truly successful people are always willing to help out. They see this as a compliment. I could not begin to tell you the number of years of mistakes I have saved in my business by using great mentors. I would be willing to bet that, without the use of my mentors, EliteFTS would not be here today and I would not be writing this book.

I am always asked, "How do you find these mentors?" This is easier than you think if you keep your eyes and ears open. They are all around you. Look for those who are successful at what you do and then seek them out. Most people I know can do this. It is the next part they have trouble with—you have to ask them! There is a skill to getting to yes, but most of you will never develop the courage to ask in the first place, so I will discuss this first. My two-year-old has no problem asking for what he wants. I remember when I was a child, I also didn't have any problem asking for what I wanted, and if I didn't get the answer I was looking for, I would find another way to ask. I would keep asking until I got what I wanted. As we become adults, we become more self-sufficient and forget to ask for help with what we would like to achieve. We think we can figure it out for ourselves. While this may be true, it would be so much faster and easier to ask those who already know. Somewhere along the line, we become afraid of the word no. So rather than being rejected, we would rather just not ask at all. The thing to remember is—what if the answer had been yes? Guess you'll never know if you do not ask in the first place.

So how do you get to the yes answer? The one thing you don't want to do is come out of the blue and ask for help with no regard for what your potential mentor does or the time he has. Do some research first. If you're seeking business advice from a company president, take the time to find some background information. Visit his or her store or Web site, talk to other employees, see if you can find any media information. Find everything you can and review it all. During this process you may find what you're looking for and not need to contact the president at all. Then again, you may find out that this is not the right company for you. Lastly, you may discover that you'll need to contact the president for more information. The next thing to do is to become a customer. When I have suggested this in the past, many people have asked me how this will make a difference. This matters for two reasons: First, the best way to really know a company is to do business with them. Second, I can almost guarantee that whoever you're trying to speak with will look you up in their database to see if you've supported their company in the past. This may not make a difference in all cases, but it sure can't hurt you any.

Coworkers—Team Members

At some point in time we all have to work with others to get a job done. You don't have to like the people you work with, but you still have to get the job done. As stated with the earlier bench press example, you're only as strong as your weakest link.

I have been a part of Westside Barbell Club for many years, and while powerlifting is an individual sport, Westside is not. For many years Westside has produced some of the strongest powerlifters in the world. These lifters do not see themselves as being any better than any of the other lifters in the club. Chuck Vogelpohl is a great example of this. Chuck is a great lifter, having squatted more than 1,000 pounds in the 220-pound weight class and was the 2004 WPO middleweight champion at the Arnold Classic. Chuck is known throughout the powerlifting world for his intense desire to be the best. What the powerlifting world does not know is how far he will go out of his way to help the lesser-known lifters in the club. He knows that Westside is only as strong as the weakest lifter, and that when Westside gets better, he gets better. I've known Chuck for many years, and I also know there have been several lifters in the club he may have not liked for various reasons, but this has never stopped him from helping them get better. It makes little difference if you don't like someone on your team—you are all after the same thing, and there is more power in the team than there is in any individual.

Your Self

What if you are the problem? What if you are the one holding the team back? What if you are holding yourself back?

Have you ever thought of this? Well, you should. Do you treat others the way you would like to be treated? Do you take the time to help your team get better? Are you a good husband or wife? Are you a good parent? How about a good friend? Do you take the time to help others who ask? Could you help make a difference in someone's life? Are you a part of someone's network? If you are not any of these things, then you must take a good look in the mirror and ask yourself: What do I need to change about myself right now to build better relationships?

Chapter Six

Criticism

* * * * * * * * * *

Do what you feel in your heart is right,
for you will be criticized anyway.

Eleanor Roosevelt

Criticism is prejudice made plausible.

H.L. Mencken

To avoid criticism, do nothing,
say nothing, and be nothing.

Elbert Hubbard

In criticism I will be bold, and as sternly,
absolutely just with a friend or foe.
From this purpose nothing shall turn me.

Edgar Allan Poe

You can't operate a company by fear,
because the way to eliminate fear is to avoid criticism.
And the way to avoid criticism is to do nothing.

Steve Ross

*I much prefer the sharpest criticism
of a single intelligent man to the
thoughtless approval of the masses.*

Johann Kepler

*A critic is a man who knows the way
but can't drive the car.*

Kenneth Tynan

*Reviewers are usually people who would
have been poets, historians, biographers, if they could.
They have tried their talents at one thing or another
and have failed; therefore they turn critic.*

Samuel Taylor Coleridge

*If they could, they would;
since they can't, they rant.*

David Tate

*It behooves every man to remember that the work
of the critic is of altogether secondary importance,
and that, in the end, progress is accomplished
by the man who does things.*

Theodore Roosevelt

Criticism (as defined by the American Heritage Dictionary):
1. The art of criticizing, especially adversely.

Critics (as defined by the American Heritage Dictionary):
1. One who forms and expresses judgments of the merits, faults, value, or truth of a matter.
2. One who tends to make harsh or carping judgments; a fault finder.

Type of Criticism

There are many types of criticism: criticism you give and criticism you get. Criticism can be constructive, understandable, natural—or hurtful.

Criticism is very damaging when it concerns *who* someone is, not what they *do*. When you give criticism, you must always keep in mind that many people can't separate what they do from what they are, and may not take your criticism in a constructive manner. If this is the case, you will become a target for them and lose any respect they may have had for you. If you give criticism, it should be constructive in nature—*or just keep your mouth shut*. You must always think about how you would feel if you were approached in the same way with the same comments. However, don't be afraid to give constructive criticism, as this is always the best advice that can be given to someone. First, ask if they would be interested in hearing your constructive criticism. If they say no, then don't worry about it, as they wouldn't listen to you anyway. If they say yes, then pour it on them—but be constructive.

Know It All

I have seen many coaches offer help to lifters in competitions, gyms, clubs, by email and telephone, only to end up irritating the athletes. The athletes become irritated because of the coaches' approach. Many athletes spend thousands of hours preparing the methods they use and don't take kindly to being told that everything they're doing is wrong. Through trial and error they've come up with a program and may not be interested in what you have to say. I was exactly the same way. I had 15 years of training under my belt and thought I had it all figured out. I also had many other teachers and coaches try to steer me to other ways of training, but all they ever did was piss me off. I might have listened if they had more than just an education background and more to offer than telling me that *everything* I was doing was wrong. How could *everything* be wrong when I had been using it for over 15 years and was a hell of a lot stronger than they were? The methods I was using were also supported by the research I was reading. When they could lift what I could *then* maybe I would listen. I thought I knew it all. What I did not know is that they all had something to offer. They just could not find the best way to communicate it to me.

Big Squat Record

One day, a powerlifting coach (Louie Simmons) walked up to me at the Toledo Hall of Fame Powerlifting Championships and asked, "Would you like to hear some advice?" Since I had just badly missed my second-attempt squat, I decided to listen. I knew of Louie from the lifters he had trained and his own accomplishments in the sport of powerlifting. Louie took a few minutes to show me how to expand and push my abdominal muscles against my belt when I squatted, and then told me he would back spot me just to make sure I remembered. When I unracked the same weight that minutes ago I couldn't even stand up with, I heard Louie talk me through the lift by yelling, "Use your belt! Hold your air!" I could not believe the difference this made, as I squatted the weight without any problem and felt like I could have squatted 50 pounds more!

Afterward, Louie asked me if I would like more advice. I said yes, and over the next few years everything I thought I knew about training changed. This change may not have happened had Louie approached me and said, "Hey your form sucks and so does your training." He knew that there is a very delicate balance between helping and upsetting, and decided to take the path that was best for me. When you choose the path that is best for the other party, success is achieved for both parties. Critics choose the path that is only best for them. They are only concerned with what will make them look better. They feel the best way for them to look better is to make others look bad. This is the way of the critic.

How I Look

I do not look like your normal small-business owner. I have a shaved head, goatee, and weigh close to 300 pounds, with body fat around 12%. I spend a very large part of my life in a weight room. In many ways you can say I grew up in a weight room. Since my junior year in high school I've been judged by the way I look. It began as "the dumb jock" and grew throughout the years to a newer, higher standard—"the dumb powerlifter." The bigger you get, the more stares you get, and you even begin to think this is kind of cool. Part of me has always wanted to become the biggest freak I could so when I walked down the street, people would stop and think, "Damn, that guy is a freak!" I have never really cared about how people perceived the way I look, but now, as a small-business owner, there are many ways this can work for and against me. For example, when I'm in a business meeting, I find I have to work harder to break free of the first impression others have of me. I have also found that when you're a lifter, you're also very confident and carry yourself differently, and this demands attention without your having to say anything. It is what you do with this attention that can make or break you. Why do I bring this up? I have learned over the years never to judge people by the way they look. When you are the victim, you see things in a different light. Have you ever noticed that when you shop in retail stores it's always the properly dressed sales reps that seem to blow you off and have an attitude? If you have, then you've probably also noticed that those who may look "different" always seem to give great service. I have received some of the best service from clerks that look like they're dressed for Halloween year round, with a zillion piercings, more tattoos than I could count, and wild-color hair.

How Do You Feel?

Do not judge people based on how they look. You have to do your best to get past this. The value of a person runs much deeper than how they look. If you find you can't get past it, and do not like them because of it, then get over it and move on. You don't have to speak to anyone, and can choose who you want and don't want to do business with. Let's face it: If this is how you really feel, then they probably wouldn't what to be around you either. I know many of you are now asking, "What do you mean? What's wrong with me?" I'm sorry, I forgot—you're perfect and everyone should be based on your standards. You are the exception to all rules and should be the model example for humankind. You have never and will never do wrong or make mistakes. You, my friend, are perfect.

So how does it feel to be judged without my knowing who you really are?

Personal Criticism

Shortly after I began powerlifting, at the young age of 14, I began to experience hurtful criticism firsthand. I write "hurtful" not because of the way it made me feel but for the way it was *intended* to make me feel. Only you can decide how you'll feel about what someone says to your face, behind your back, and now, in the digital age, behind their keyboard. Was I criticized before the age of 14? Yes, of course I was, but I didn't care as much because it was about things I really didn't care about in the first place, as you will see later in this chapter. I was called a slow learner, stupid, the list goes on and on, but it didn't make me as upset as being criticized for something I loved to do. I don't know many people who really care about being criticized for something they suck at in the first place. Ask me to paint you a picture, and guess what? It will suck and you can tell me so—because I don't care. Now criticize a 14-year-old's dedication to powerlifting and start rumors ranging from lying about the weights he lifts to drug use and you'll find one pissed-off kid. Over the years, I have gotten much stronger, my lifts have all gone way up, my ranking has gone up, I have become much smarter, and have had great success in all areas of my life. As I have grown as a person, so has the criticism. Criticism has been there through the good times and the bad. When you're striving for success, it will always be there. There's just no way around it. The key is to know what and whom to listen to and avoid all the rest.

I Remember

As mentioned before, I was criticized (or made fun of) throughout my entire preschool and middle-school years. I was labeled in my early school years as a "slow learner" or, as they called it back then, someone with a "learning disability." As with most kids, I can't remember everything about my preschool years, but I do remember a this:

- I remember having a huge picture of a clock on my desk, with the hour and minute hands pointing to the exact time I had to leave the classroom to see my tutor. I hated this clock picture. I was the only one in the room that had this plastered on his desk. The only good part was that I got to leave and go to a very small, private room and work with flash cards. When I did a good job, I would get a cool sticker to put on my shirt, and if I did a *really* good job, I would get candy as a reward.

- I remember being made fun of on the playground for being stupid and always being picked close to last for all the team activities.

- I remember great sunny days at the local swimming pool with my friends and having to leave early to go see my special-education teacher.

- I remember having to take special classes through middle school and wondering why all my neighborhood friends were in more advanced classes.

- I remember all my high school friends being tracked for college-prep classes while I was taking classes such as earth science, basic reading, business math, etc.

- I remember being told I would not be able to handle those other classes.

- I remember being told my GPA would not be high enough to graduate high school and that I may have to take summer classes.

- I remember the way 90% of the teachers and administration treated me. If it were not for football, the other 10% would have also treated me the same way—like a moron.

- I remember taking freshman college-prep classes as a senior in an attempt to get into college.

- I remember being turned down by every college I applied to except for one very small business university in Tiffin, Ohio.

- I remember spending my entire first year in college taking classes that were not for credit. These classes were to make up all the classes I should have taken in high school, including algebra, English, biology, speaking, and history.

- I remember passing all my classes and being around people who didn't know I was supposed to be stupid. I began to believe that maybe I wasn't a slow learner and actually had a chance to learn something.

- I remember leaving the small business university to attended Bowling Green State University.

- I remember flunking out of BGSU after my first quarter. I failed all my classes except for one D in earth science. I guess it was a good thing I had taken this in high school.

- I remember going back home for the spring thinking about what I had been told my whole life— "You're not college material."

The Change

You may be asking, "Why are you telling me all this?" Why would you expose your past in such a negative way? I didn't have a bad childhood. I grew up in a strong middle-class family that cared and still does care very much for one another. I grew up with very strong family values. My parents did a very good job raising my two brothers, sister, and me to be strong, independent adults who knew the difference between right and wrong. If I can be as good a parent to my kids as they were to me, then I know I'll be very successful. My parents had their work cut out for them, as they had been told my entire childhood that their son was "slow," had "attention deficient disorder," and many other things. As a parent, what are you to do? They did the best they could do. They hired help, worked with me when ever they could, and hoped for the best. The truth finally came to a head in the parking lot of my old high school weight room. I was home from college for the spring. I would have rather stayed at Bowling Green, but as you remember—I didn't really have a choice. I was trying to find a job at the time and had given up on the whole college thing. My parents were pressuring me to go back, but I had had enough of it. I was not a smart kid and college was not for me. I figured I could just stay in town and find a nice factory job that paid well. As with most other times in my life, I was training for an upcoming powerlifting competition and thought I would go back to the old high school weight room for a training session. It had been a year and a half since I had been there, and I needed a change of pace from the gym I was training at. My brother was a junior at the time and was conditioning for the following football season. He had a training session with the team, making it easy for me to gain access to the weight room. After my training session I made my way back to my car to get a bottle of Gatorade I had bought on the way to the school. As I leaned against the car I saw one of my old coaches walk out the gym doors and head my way.

Coach Shoop

Bill Shoop was one of my football coaches in junior high school. I always liked coach Scoop because he was also a weightlifter and would always run around yelling out intense things like, "Rip or be ripped!" He was a very intense coach and very passionate when it came to helping us be our best. I loved his coaching style and how he could get the team fired up. Unlike other coaches, he didn't try and take the limelight and gave every kid all he had. If you were a starter you got his best; if you were a bench warmer, you got his best. His best was all he had to give, and he gave it to everyone. He would always tell me about how he just bench pressed some huge weight for multiple reps earlier in the day. I shared the same passion for training and always made it a goal to be stronger than him some day. This kept me training hard in the weight room, and during my senior year I did become stronger than him.

Coach Shoop didn't see you for what you were but for what you could be. I didn't really understand what this would mean for me personally until years later, drinking that Gatorade outside my high school weight room. I was leaning back against my car sucking down a bottle when Coach walked toward me. He asked how I was doing, and I went into a long dialogue about how I was training for an upcoming meet and how my squat had really taken off over the past year. I told him about all the training research I had been looking into and what things I had applied with success and what things did not work out so well. I let him in on a few bench pressing tips I had picked up over the past year and how, if he used a few of them, he might be able to get his bench press to go up 30 or 40 pounds.

Do You Want to Know What I Think?

We spoke training for the next five or 10 minutes, and then he asked me how school was going. I guess he didn't know what had happened, and I had enough respect for him to tell him the truth. I told him how I went to Tiffin for a year and then transferred to BGSU and flunked all but one of my classes and was asked to sit out a semester. He went on to ask me if I was going back in the summer or fall. I told him that I didn't plan on going back and that college was not made for people like me. About this time he leaned back against his truck that was parked next to mine and asked me one question I will never forget.

"Dave, do you want to know what I think?"

What was I supposed to say? Here was a guy I had respected since the day I met him. I respected him enough to just spend 10 minutes telling him all my training secrets. He looked me in the face and said:

"Dave, you are not stupid, you have never been stupid—you're just lazy and do not care."

I didn't know what to think. I'm lazy! What is he talking about? I bust my ass in the weight room every day. I'm not some bum who stays home watching TV and eating chips all day. I do not care! I care more about my training than anything else. I eat clean, don't smoke, don't drink, and will not do anything that could hurt my training results in any way. I think he could tell my frustration as he went on.

"Look, I understand you've been tracked and labeled your entire life as being a slow learner. The school systems have a way of placing people in different career tracks and only go on what they feel is best for the kid. There are a few ways to be tracked, including business, shop, college prep, and 'just graduate.' Have you ever considered they may have been wrong?"

"Look, I see what you're saying," I replied, "but I've never been good at school since day one." I then went on to share some of the stories listed earlier in my "I remember" list. The difference was that he couldn't care less about what I was saying and actually told me:

"Dave, excuses are like assholes and they all stink."

You Do Not Care Enough to Try

This statement drove the point home. He went on to tell me how I had just spent 10 minutes telling him very detailed training information I had collected from books and journals. I had found the information, read the information, retained the information, and then applied the information. He told me that I already had all the skills I needed—I just wasn't using them for my other courses of study. If I placed half the effort into my classes as I did my training, then I would be an "A" student. It all came down to the fact that I did not care enough and was too lazy to try. He told me that I might have to work twice as hard as the next guy to get the same results, but that was my reality—*which nobody cares about.* Nobody cares how hard it will be for you; they only care about the end result.

The Long Drive

After we finished speaking I got into my car and drove around for the next hour thinking about the things he said. Was he right? Was I just lazy? I knew I didn't care because I skipped most of my classes. I even skipped one of the finals because I had no idea what was going on and figured the time would be better spent in the gym. Could I have been tracked wrong? Could the school system have made a mistake? Did it matter, or am I living with false beliefs that were established years ago? Does it matter now? How come I can retain all this training information? These and hundreds of other questions kept going through my mind for the next hour. Finally, I realized what I had to do.

Going Back

When I got home I let my parents know I was going back for summer classes and finish what I had started. I still didn't like BGSU, and it took me five more years to get my GPA up high enough to graduate. This could have happened faster if I had retaken the courses I failed, but this was one risk I was not willing to take. I also had a way to make sure I didn't fail any more classes. I wanted to go to the University of Toledo but needed a 2.5 to transfer. This became my goal. I would also take only those classes that interested me. I did not use any type of career track. I just flipped through the course catalog and took what seemed interesting. Yes, I know this is not the best way to go through college, but I was not taking any chances on my GPA. After nine more semesters I transferred to the University of Toledo and set up a bachelor of science track curriculum on the goal of being a strength and conditioning coach. They didn't have anything like this at the time, so we set up a program based on the courses that would help me the most. Some of these included nutritional biochemistry, anatomy, philosophy, psychology, motor learning, exercise physiology, sports mechanics, and biomechanics. I'm not going to lie to you: I also went back and retook the two classes I failed my first semester at BGSU. I didn't have to take them again—it was just something I felt I needed to do. After another two years I received my degree with close to a 3.5 GPA. I also received A's in both the classes that sent me home from BGSU years earlier. I now see failing those classes as one of the best things that ever happened to me. If I hadn't flunked out, I wouldn't have been in the parking lot that day. Up until that point in my life just getting by was good enough, after that day I knew I had to change my way of thinking.

I know the true strength of a man is not in how much he can lift but how high he can lift others. I may have beat Coach's bench press, but I still aspire to be the man who helped me that day in the parking lot.

Critics Revisited

Was Bill Shoop a critic? Yes, he was a critic who had a plan to help—not destroy. If you're going to criticize someone, make sure you can also offer a plan of action. If not, *keep your mouth shut*. I was told two things that were very hard to hear: that I was lazy and did not care. If that had been all I was told, it would have pissed me off and not made me drive around for one hour thinking it over. I was also told and shown how I had the skills but was not using them. There was my solution. When you're presented with criticism—and with a solution—from those you respect: LISTEN. You may not like what you hear, but take some time and think it over. I'm not telling you to do what they say, but think about it and do what's best for you. When you're at a crossroads, what you decide to do can and will make a profound difference in your life. If you're offered advice from someone who has been there and seen it all before, I suggest you take some time and really think about what you've been told.

If you're criticized, and no positive advice is offered, then forget it and get on with your life. Those who try to tear down without any plan to build up are only trying to make themselves look better and could care less about you. They're looking for you to get upset for their own gratification. This is a game of win/lose. If you get upset, they win and you lose. If you blow it off, they'll try harder but will always lose in the long run. You're too busy getting things done to worry about those who can't finish anything.

Final Quote

Here is one of my all-time favorite quotes:

It is not the critic who counts, not the man who points out how the strong man stumbled, or where the doer of deeds could have done better. The credit belongs to the man who is actually in the arena; who's face is marred by sweat and blood; who strives valiantly; who errs and come up short again and again because there is no effort without error and shortcoming; who knows the great enthusiasms, the great devotion, spends himself in a worthy cause; who at his best knows in the end the triumph of high achievement; and who at worst, if he fails, at least fails while daring greatly, so that his place shall never be with those cold timid souls who have never tasted victory or defeat.

Theodore Roosevelt

Chapter Seven

Education

*Apply yourself, Get all the education
you can, but then ... do something.
Don't just stand there.
Make it happen.*

Lee Iacocca

*Your biggest opportunity probably
lies under your own feet,
in your current job, industry,
education, experiences, or interests.*

Brian Tracy

*The things I want to know are in books;
my best friend is the man who'll
get me a book I ain't read.*

Abraham Lincoln

If someone is going down the wrong road,
he doesn't need motivation to speed him up.
What he needs is education to turn him around.

Jim Rohn

I have never let my schooling
interfere with my education.

Mark Twain

If you are planning for a year, sow rice;
if you are planning for a decade, plant trees;
if you are planning for a lifetime,
educate people.

Chinese proverb

Education is what you get
when you read the fine print.
Experience is what you get
when you don't.

Pete Seeger

A truly wise man uses few words;
a person with understanding
is even tempered.

Proverbs 17:22

Education (as defined by the American Heritage Dictionary):

1. The act or process of educating or being educated.
2. The knowledge or skill obtained or developed by a learning process.
3. An instructive or enlightening experience.

Know It all

From the first day I touched a weight, I became obsessed with learning more about how to become bigger and stronger. I would walk to the bookstore once a week and buy up all the new books and magazines I could find. Every dollar I made would be invested in these books and magazines. This passion continued through my high school and college years. I spent countless hours in the library, making copies from journals, magazines, books, and whatever else I could find. I studied strength and conditioning, biochemistry, exercise science, nutrition, psychology—if it could help me get stronger, I read it. I know I've read more than 1,000 books in my pursuit of strength. If it was in print, I found it and read it. I also spoke with everyone I felt could help me with my pursuit of strength. After many years of study and training, I believed I knew all I had to know. My studies had come to the point where I was not reading anything new but just the same material over and over. Even the people I spoke to were all telling me pretty much the same things. At this point, I began to close myself off to other people's ideas. Who were they to tell me? I had read more and spent more time in the weight room than they had. How could they know something I didn't know? I was wrong.

Lesson Learned

My problem was that all my education was not doing anything for me. My lifts were not going up; in fact, they stayed the same for five years. I just couldn't break out of my rut. I figured all I had to do was keep doing the same things I had been doing, and sooner or later I would have my day. I had my day all right, but it was not the day I was looking for. It was one of the worst, most disastrous lifting days of my life. Little did I know that it would also turn out to be one of the most important events of my life.

At the Circleville, Ohio, Bench Press Championships, during my second-attempt bench press, I felt a strong pop from my left pectoral muscle. I suddenly lost all function of my arm and the 500-pound barbell came crashing down on me. I survived the accident but was left with a torn right pectoris major. My pec doubled in size and there was now a huge indentation between my front deltoid and where my chest used to be. The muscle had rolled up and begun to swell. There was no pain, as the tendon was torn off the bone, but I knew something was wrong. At this time, Louie Simmons, the coach of the world-famous Westside Barbell Club (known for producing the strongest powerlifters in the world), came up to me and said, "If you don't change your ways, you will be out of this sport very fast." To me, I was already out. I was going to graduate from college in one month and had not made any progress in my training for the past five years. After a few more conversations with Louie, and a successful surgery, I realized I didn't know anything about training. I had to learn more.

Driving Force

Louie introduced me to a whole other level of training information I had never heard of. I began reading Russian training manuals and spent countless hours discussing training with Louie. I decided to move to Columbus, Ohio, train under Louie, and be a part of Westside Barbell. To this day, I still call Westside home. I've still yet to meet one person who knew more about making athletes strong than Louie. It was meeting him that taught me two very important lessons about education:

1. No matter how much you think you know, there is much more to learn.

2. Know whom you are listening to and make sure they're qualified.

These two lessons have been the driving force behind my own education. When I founded Elitefts.com, I knew right away that I had to become very educated in business, and from my experience with training, I knew exactly what to do: I started reading everything I could find on small-business development. I created a network with other successful small-business owners. I hired a business consultant and invested heavily in education. During the first three years, all the profit of the company was invested in seminars, books, tapes, and other educational materials. Because of the lessons I learned "under the bar," I was able to take a company that started with less than a shoestring budget and grow it into a successful, thriving organization.

Unreal Data

Education is still a driving force in my life, as I read between two and three books a week and am always scanning journals, magazines, newsletters, and other material to find information relative to what I'm working on at the time. The numbers of people who do not take advantage of the great education that's available in this country astound me. I just read that according to the American Booksellers Association, 80% of Americans don't buy a single book in a given year, and 70% haven't been in a bookstore in the same time period. Fifty-eight percent of Americans haven't read a book past high school, and 52% of college graduates haven't read a single book past graduation.

Statistics also show that only 14% of Americans will walk into a bookstore or library and walk out with a book, while only 10% will read past the first chapter.

I've found several practices that have made a huge difference in my training, business, and life. I know for a fact that when exercised, these practices—or habits—will also make a huge difference for you. You don't need to use every one, even though it wouldn't be a bad idea. Just use what you can for four weeks, and you'll be surprised at the results.

1. Invest in Your Education

Treat your education as an investment in yourself. With strength training, you get back what you put in. Imagine your goal is to bench press 500 pounds, yet you never went into the gym to train. The same is true with your education. Just because you're no longer in school doesn't mean you never have to read again. In fact, you need to read and study harder if you want to be successful in training, business, and life. I've invested 5%–10% of my net income each year on education ever since I can remember, and I can say that this investment has paid back far more than any other investment I've made. The person you will be in the next five years is dependent upon the books you read and the people you meet. With this in mind, why not seek out the best education you can that can help you become the person you want to be?

"But I don't have any extra money to become more educated," you say? Bull! All that tells me is you're too lazy or don't care to make yourself better. If you break down what you spend your money on, you'll be amazed at how much of it goes into activities that have nothing to do with advancing your goals. While I'm at it, don't tell me you don't have time to devote to education. This is also crap. If you drive, you can listening to audiobooks. You can also turn the damn TV off and pick up a book. Basically, you can spend less time "doing nothing" and more time "doing something."

Turn off the TV and open a book. You will be amazed at what this can do for you.

2. Buy the Book

I suggest you always buy the book instead of checking it out of the library or borrowing it from a friends. When you buy the book, you own the book. When you own the book, you can mark it up. Always read with a pen in hand. Underline, highlight, and make notes on anything you think may have an impact on your life. I have many books that are so full of notes, different highlighter colors, underlines, and Post-it notes. I find myself always going back through many of my books to find an idea or to be reminded of something I read in the past.

Buy your books, and they'll keep giving back to you for a lifetime.

3. Rip and Read

One of the best things I've done for my education over the years is to keep a reading file. In this file, I keep all the information I want for reading at a later time. I keep this file with me at all times, as you never know when you may have five or ten free minutes to catch up. The key to this file is to place only *relevant* information in it. If you're reading a magazine, go straight to the table of contents and see what articles will help you work toward your goals. Once you find the articles you want, go straight to them and rip them out of the magazine. Don't keep the magazine sitting to read later. Get what you need, rip it out, file it, and move on. The same is true with information found online. There are thousands of Web sites with plenty of information you can use. When you find something, print it out and place it in your reading file. Many of you will bookmark the site—then forget what site it was that you saw the information you're looking for.

Once you read the information in your reading file, either file it somewhere else or toss it. Don't keep it in your reading file, as you've already read it, and it will just clutter the file. It also helps to highlight or underline the information in the article that you find the most useful. This way, if you have to come back to it later, you won't have to re-read the entire document to find what you're looking for.

"Rip and read" is the key to getting through the most relevant information in the fastest time.

4. Learn from Experts

One thing I didn't pay attention to early on was whom I was listening to. I just devoured all the strength-training information I could find and never took the time to see who was behind the information. When I became more involved in the educational aspect of the industry, I found some very amazing things. For example, there are many fitness writers who don't even train! Many coaches who don't train! Many trainers who don't train! Yet, they're all writing articles on how we all should train! I couldn't believe what I was seeing. The most disturbing thing is that readers see these authors as experts because they're in print. I've found this to be true in all areas, not just strength and conditioning. So when I began reading to grow my business, I remembered the lesson I learned from my strength and conditioning background and always checked out the background on the authors of the books I was reading. If I wanted to read a book on marketing, I'd go to the author's Web site. If the site sucked, then I knew the author didn't practice what he or she preached.

Find out who you feel the expects are in the field you wish to study, then check to see if they really are who they say they are.

5. One Hour

We're all busy, but the last time I checked, we all have the same 24 hours a day. We can all find time to read each day. If you say you don't have the time, then let me give you some ideas on how to find the time.

- Get up one hour earlier.
- Stay up one hour later.
- Cut back on TV time.
- Read during your lunch break.
- Carry articles with you to read during slow times of the day.

In other words, look closely at your day and I bet you'll find time to read. If you were told that you had to read an hour a day or you'd die within the next seven days, *you'd find the time.* You may not die in the next seven days, but your life can greatly be enhanced when your education is enhanced.

In many ways, you can say your life does depend on your education.

6. Don't Loan It

Don't loan out your books, because they'll never get back to you again. What's worse is that you can loan it out to help someone else, and 99% of the time, that person will never read it. You try to save your friend a few bucks and end up buying the book again at a later time. Here is a great example. The book *Supertraining* by Mel C. Siff is one of the best books ever written in the field of strength and conditioning. Many years ago, I went through this book with a highlighter and marked all the best parts. Over the years, I've written notes in the margins and underlined sections. This book looked like it had been destroyed by a two-year-old with a box of crayons and a fine-point pen. I can't begin to count the number of times I had gone through that text but would have to guess it's in the hundreds. That is, until the day I loaned it to another trainer to look over. He was thinking of buying the book and wanted to review it first. I saw this as a sales opportunity, since this is one of the titles we sell at Elitefts.com. After a few weeks, I asked for it back and was told he had lent it to someone else. Now, 10 years later, I still don't have my book back. The trainer didn't even buy the book, so I'm not only out the sale but had to buy a new copy for myself. At $55 a book I was now out over $100. The price of a new book is not the biggest cost of my loss. There is no way to put a price tag on my notes and highlights in the book. Yes, I have a new copy but it's just not the same as the original. There are many other books that have disappeared from my collection, and when I go to replace them, I find many are out of print. If you really want to help your "book stealers" out—tell them to buy their own!

If you have my original copy of *Supertraining*, I want it back!

7. Buy Tons of Books

If you see a book you like, buy it. If you read a review about a book you like, buy it. If someone tells you about a book, buy it. If you see a book mentioned in another book you're reading that's very good, buy it. I've found great books in many places: old, beat-up bookstores, referrals in articles and other books, conversations with people I respect, related book lists, best-seller lists, etc. Always be on the lookout, and when you do find a good lead, buy the book before you forget about it. This is one place where the Internet works great. I can click on a book at Amazon.com in less than 10 seconds. Three days later, it's at my door. Other great places to find good books are industry-specific Web sites like ours at Elitefts.com. We review each book to ensure the information will be helpful and don't place any book on our cart that doesn't pass our review. This way, we take the research into our own hands so our customers always get a higher-quality product. Smaller companies will also carry the smaller self-published books that usually have the best information but never make it to the large booksellers' shelves.

8. Learn to Pre-read

This very simple skill will save you hours of reading time. When you begin to read a book, take the time to read the inside book jacket to get an idea of who's writing the material. Next, move to the table of contents and check to see if you really need to read the entire book or if there are only a few areas you really need to focus on now. From there, read the foreword to gain a better insight as to why the book was written. Finally, skim the book, page by page, chapter by chapter, to get a feel for the contents. If you see a section that can really help you right then and there, dog-ear it or place a Post-it note on it, then come back to it when you begin reading. After you finish this process, you'll already have a very good feel for what the book is about and where to find the information you're looking for. Go straight to what you need and read it first. This is why you got the book in the first place.

9. Audio books/seminars/videos EST.

There are many other ways to increase your education. I'm a big fan of audiobook programs. We all spend a great deal of time in our cars that can be spent learning. I know many people who spend more than three hours a day in their car. Think of how much they could learn if they used this 21 hours a week to better educate themselves. You can now find audiobooks on just about any subject you like.

Seminars are also a great way to advance your goals. At Elitefts. com, we have given hundreds of seminars on strength training and seen attendants break through sticking points they had been dealing with for years. The information presented at seminars is very often the most advanced information on the market. There are seminars on every topic you can think of. With a little research, you can always find what you're looking for.

Videos and DVDs also offer many great advantages. It's easy and cheap to put together a DVD or video today, so we're now beginning to see these products coming from great underground sources you would not hear about any other way. You'll find many of these in the strength and conditioning industry, with small gyms putting together training videos of information you may never have seen before. The quality of the product may not be the best, but the information you receive far exceeds any higher-quality production.

Look for education everywhere. You can find gems in places you'd never think of.

Chapter Eight

Risk Management

*It is impossible to win the race
unless you venture to run,
impossible to win a victory
unless you dare a battle.*

Richard M. De Vos

*Accept the challenges,
so that you may feel
the exhilaration of victory.*

General George S. Patton

*Courage is what it takes to
stand up and speak.
Courage is also what it takes to
sit down and listen.*

Unknown

*Courage is the first of
human qualities because
it is the quality which
guarantees all others.*

W. Churchill

*Our greatest glory is not in never falling,
but in rising every time we fall.*

Confucius

Talk does not cook rice.

Chinese proverb

*The difference between a successful person
and others is not a lack of strength,
not a lack of knowledge,
but rather a lack of will.*

Vince Lombardi

*Courage is not the lack of fear;
it is acting in spite of it.*

Mark Twain

Risk (as defined by the American Heritage Dictionary):
1. The possibility of suffering harm or loss; danger.
2. A factor, thing, element, or course involving uncertain danger.
3. One considered with respect to the possibility of loss.

Five Types of Risk

Creating an outline for this article turned out to be more difficult than for the other articles in this book. To be blunt: Risk can make or break you. There are many types of risks you can take, and trying to organize them clearly is not as easy as you may think. Through my research on this topic, I came across an article by Brian Tracy, called "Taking Smart Risks." In it, Brian outlined five types of risks:

1. The risk you do not take.
2. Unnecessary risk.
3. Risk you can afford to take.
4. Risk you can't afford to take.
5. Risk you can't afford NOT to take.

While reading Brian's article, I was reminded of how I was confronted with these five types of risk "under the bar" and how they have stayed with me through the success of Elitefts.com. Taking smart and educated risks is a key factor in your success in the weight room, business, and life. Most of us are very aware of the risks we take in the weight room and understand when we can push it and when we must back off. Now we must take what we have learned and use it outside the weight room, in other areas of our life. However, there are still many of us who can use a reminder of the risk management associated with the weight room. Gaining a better understanding of the five types of risk can make a huge difference in what happens with your training.

The Risk You Do Not Take

You all know how this goes. You hear about some new jacked-up powerlifting equipment or training method. You would like to give it a shot, but your training is going great and you don't see the need to change something that's already working so well. So you do the next best thing. You find someone else to try it for you, and then you wait and see how it works out. On the other side of this issue is the lifter who's too quick to take the risk without looking at all variables. I see this all the time with powerlifting gear, especially bench-press shirts. Lifter A has been training with his new bench shirt for the past 12 weeks, then three weeks before the meet he decides to switch back to his old brand of shirt and give it a test run—only to find that his form has changed to suit the shirt he had been training in. Going back to the old brand is a risk he did not have to take and should have held off until after the meet. There are a number for people out there who always want to have the next greatest thing on the market and want it as soon as it comes out. This is great and should be commended, but timing has to be taken into consideration.

Let's look at it from another perspective. I've been reading and hearing about how great static ISO training is for strength development. Rather then dump what I've been doing and jumping on the bandwagon, I've been sitting back to see some of the real results, especially results specific to my own training needs. So I've decided not to take the risk, because I don't have to. I know there will be hundreds of other lifters who will jump in and test it out. As it happens, it's a good thing I waited, because the results have not been there, and my training has advanced each week, while those who tested this method have not made the same progress I have. This was a risk I didn't have to take to advance my training.

The Unnecessary Risk

The unnecessary risks are those that will not have any impact on the goals you're trying to achieve and more than likely will not move you closer to them. These are the risks that may seem important to one party but are not as important to the other. A great example is our current software situation at Elitefts.com. We'd been running a few different business systems that had been working well for us with some exceptions. A few months ago I decided to take a look at a few new programs designed for Internet mail-order businesses. There were a few I found very interesting that could help us solve some problems we were having with accounts receivable, sales, and inventory. As with everything these days, these solutions were all very expensive. Naturally, the sales representatives were pushing very hard for us to make the switch to their software solutions, saying that we could not function effectively without them. The one thing I did know is that sales were slow in the summer, steel prices were going up, and the holiday season was coming and would require us to stock up our inventory. I also knew that expenses were not going to drop with the sales, and that the new system would take time to generate extra revenue, if it would at all. I finally realized that it was unnecessary to make this decision now and was best left to a later time. After further analysis, we also created new in-house solutions to our problems without having to spend a dime. Had I taken the risk without future research, we would now be having serious cash-flow problems.

Training is much the same. If things are going good and some-one suggests you try something new, you need to take stock of where you're at, what you could possibly gain, and what you could possibly lose if it didn't work out. If you don't do this, the outcome could lead to disastrous results, resulting in overtrain-ing, undertraining, loss of technical skills, or injury.

Risk You Can Afford to Take

This is the best risk of all. Let's say that money is not an issue and you're 16 weeks out from your next powerlifting competition and would like to try out the new metal Viking gear. This is no problem: All you have to do is place the order, wait for the gear, and give it a shot. If it works as well for you as it has for others, then you made the right choice; if it doesn't work for you, then no big deal— give EliteFTS a call and we'll be more than happy to refund your money (as long as you didn't trash the gear). So the risk is very minimal, and you can afford it because you're try-ing the new gear far enough in advance of your meet that you will have time to train in it and perfect the groove of the gear.

Risk You Can't Afford to Take

Training for any competition is full of risks you should and should not take. A great example is the last heavy bench session I had before my last meet. My training had been going great and I was breaking PRs left and right the whole cycle. While working up with my shirt on this particular day, I began to feel my right pec tighten up. I worked up to 575 for a single and wanted to finish the day at 635. Based on how I felt and how my training had been going, I decided that the next set was a risk I could not afford to take that close to the meet, so I called it a day. I see many lifters and athletes in this situation who choose to press on and then have to pull out of the competition because of something stupid they did 10 days out. I strongly believe that if you haven't done your training correctly up to the last 10 days before a meet, then there is nothing you can do that will help you gain more than you already have, except rest. There is nothing you can do training-wise that will make you that much stronger—but there's a hell of a lot you can do that can make you weaker or injured.

Risk You Can't Afford NOT to Take

I have trained in a denim bench shirt for the past 12 years and have always thought that such a shirt was the way to go. The problem: I've seen lifters get crazy carry-overs (a carry over is how much extra weight the gear will allow you to lift) out of their shirts, and I was getting only 80 pounds. (This may seem like a lot for some, but I know guys who get 300!) I figured if I was not getting 250 out of my shirt, then I had better get to work. So I decided to focus only on learning the shirt and perfecting my technique in the shirt. This was going to be at the expense of many things I know make me stronger. So for the time being, things like triceps work had to go on the back burner. I know that to get 160 pounds stronger on the bench is hard as hell to do and requires a ton of work, but to get 160 pounds stronger with a shirt that works would take only a fraction of this time. Being that I have an intensive injury history and have access to any metal shirt I would need, I decided that this was a risk I could not afford NOT to take. I still have some work to do, but within three months of working with my Viking shirt, I almost made a competition bench of 700—which would have been a 90-pound personal record and a 240-pound carry-over. Being that I missed the weight short of lockout on one arm and had a hell of a time getting the weight to touch, I still need to risk a bit more, but not at the expenses of the extra strength work I had given up over the past three months.

Risk or Risk Not

One of the reasons this has been one of the hardest "under the bar" stories to write is that it's difficult to illustrate types of risk with personal stories—especially when it comes to telling about when a huge risk you can't afford to take proves to be the one risk you can't afford NOT to take. The best example I can think of for this dilemma is a board-press session I had a few months ago. We were all using a one-board press to get a gauge of where we were. (The one board is a standard 2x8 cut at 12 inches in length. To do this you basically bench press while someone holds the board on you chest. This has always been the same or very close to what I can bench in a meet.) My best at the time was 605, and I would have been happy with 615. This was also my second time in my Viking bench shirt, and the 605 was with my double denim (this shirt was not a metal denim but one I felt worked very well for me). As we worked up, things felt great and I had the groove of the shirt down. I worked up to 635 and killed the weight. As far as I was concerned, I was done for the day. This was a great PR and I couldn't see any benefit to going up any higher, as my goal for the next meet was going to be right around 635.

That was all good until my training partners (Jim Wendler and Todd Brock) got on me to take another weight. They convinced me to take one more lift, and I felt 655 would be a good place to jump to. Jim politely informed me that he would not help lift the bar out and spot anything less than 700 pounds. Then Todd started in, and I began to feel put on the spot. I didn't want to look like a chump, so I agreed. I also can't lie: My real intention was to lower the weight to the board and have them pull it off. What the hell else can you think when you're faced with a 95-pound PR? As I got ready to bench, I switched modes and figured if I was going to try this, then I was going to make damn sure I gave it everything I had plus some. So after a few smelling salts, kicking over a few board-press boards, and ranting like a madman, I made the weight. It was after this lift that I started looking to a 700 pound competitive lift instead of 635 At this point 635 was now a joke to me and nothing under 700 would do.

Too Bad, Get Over It

The key to risk is how well you manage it and are able to keep it in proper perspective. You have to risk being successful, but this doesn't mean you have to take stupid risks. You have to know when to risk and not to risk. But when you feel it's time not to risk, you need to ask yourself why. If all you ever do is take risks within your comfort zone, then you'll continue to just continue as you've been going. You have to take some big risks to move forward, and you know what? Many of those big risks will not work out for you. As a matter of fact, most of the time they won't. For all those who say, "I know what you're saying, but the last time I put it on the line, I got hurt," my response is, "Too bad! Tough shit! Get over it!" I don't care about what didn't work for you or what hurt you or whatever. All I care about is what can work for you, and not risking will never get you where you want to be. Complaining about what you don't have, or the strength you wish you did have, is all bullshit and a total waste of your time (as well as the time of anyone else you share it with). Find out what you want and go after it. If you're faced with a decision that places you out of your comfort zone, then manage the risk and move on.

Chapter Nine

Perseverance

*The difference between a successful person and others
is not a lack of strength, not a lack of knowledge,
but rather a lack of will.*

Vince Lombardi

*I have missed more than 9,000 shots in my career.
I've lost almost 300 games. Twenty-six times,
I've been trusted to take the game-winning shot
and missed. I've failed over and over in my life.
And that is why I succeed.*

Michael Jordan

*I firmly believe that any man's finest hour—his greatest
fulfillment to all he holds dear—is that moment when
he has worked his heart out in a good cause and lies
exhausted on the field of battle—victorious.*

Vince Lombardi

Our greatest glory is not in never falling,
but in rising every time we fall.

Confucius

I have been driven to my knees by the overwhelming
conviction that I had nowhere else to go.

Abraham Lincoln

It is not the size of the dog in the fight,
it's the size of the fight in the dog.

Mark Twain

Don't let what you cannot do interfere
with what you can do.

John Wooden

Courage is not the lack of fear.
It is acting in spite of it.

Mark Twain

You gain strength, courage and confidence by every
experience in which you really stop to look fear in
the face. You are able to say to yourself, "I have lived
through this horror. I can take the next thing that comes
along." You must do the thing you think you cannot do.

Eleanor Roosevelt

How you ever gonna know
What it's like to live there
How you ever gonna know victory
How you ever gonna know
What it's like when dreams become reality
How you ever gonna know
How it feels to hold her
How you ever gonna know
What it's like to dance
How you ever gonna know
If you never take a chance

Garth Brooks from the song
"How You Ever Gonna Know"

Perseverance (as defined by the American Heritage Dictionary):

1. Steady persistence in adhering to a course of action, a belief, or a purpose; steadfastness.

The Baby

Who ever said life was easy? This has to be one of the dumbest things I've ever heard. Easy for who? The truth is, life can be a bitch regardless of who you are. Everyone has tough times. Just the other day someone told me life is so easy for kids: They don't have to work, pay bills, or deal with the other stresses of life. All I could think to myself is, "Oh really?" Then I told her that I have a nine-month-old at home and life is far from easy for him. I bet he would gladly trade places with her. She rolled her eyes and could not believe what I was saying. Then I asked her to imagine going to a foreign country where she did not understand a bit of the language, where she had to crawl everywhere she wanted to go, could not dress herself, had to wear a diaper, could not speak to tell anyone what she wanted, gums always hurt because of teeth tearing through them, had to drink out of a bottle, and had to eat pretty much the same stuff every day. Now tell me—how bad is your life really? You think you have problems? Her reply: "That's different. He's just a baby and does not know any better." I then told her maybe they don't know better, but they deal with it and keep moving forward. Not only that, but they also spend the rest of the time with a huge grin on their face and are as happy as anyone on this earth could be. They do not rehash how bad things are, over and over, all day long. They have no choice but to move forward—quitting is not an option. It takes a few years to learn that skill. We are all brought into this world with a very strong desire for persistence. How many times did you fall down before you walked? The correct answer is, "Until I began to walk." It does not matter how many times you fall but how many more times you get up. Life can be hard—it's supposed to be. To accomplish your goals and be successful you have to have a very strong desire to keep moving forward and never quit when the road gets tough.

Twisted

It was a cold winter Sunday afternoon. As with most Sundays during the football season, I would watch a few quarters of football on TV and then make my way outside to join up with the corner football game. There was always something going on: football during football season, basketball, baseball, soccer all year round. You could find yourself with 10 other kids knocking each other around. The ages of the kids could range from 16 down to seven or eight. It did not matter how old you were, only if you could play the game. This really didn't matter either, as new rules were being invented all the time.

I could not have been more than six or seven years old and was one of the smaller guys in the group. I still remember how cold it was, and I was all dressed up for the occasion. I had my huge winter coat, hat, gloves, and the rubber boots that went over my tennis shoes. I still have no idea why I had to wear bread bags around my feet as well, but I was ready to go. I was so jacked up in clothes that I looked like the little boy from *A Christmas Story*. The game was going very well and the extra clothes turned out to be a great thing, as I could not feel how hard the ground was after getting smashed by kids twice my size. A few plays later, as I was running across the yard, I tripped over a sewer-drain hole and twisted my ankle. The pain was unreal; I thought I had broken my ankle. I left the game right away and made my way home. My dad was still sitting in his chair watching the game as I made my way crying into the house and stripped off my winter gear. My mom asked me what had happened. I told her I had broken my ankle on the sewer drain. My dad called me into the family room and asked to see how bad it was. I hobbled over his way and proceeded to take my boots off. After a minute of him tugging and twisting my ankle, he told me to put my winter gear back on and go back out to the game. I told him again that I had a broken ankle and could not walk. I was informed that I had only twisted my ankle and that I needed to go back outside, walk it off ,and get back in the game. Once more I told him that I could not walk. "Go back, walk it off, and get back in the game!" I put my coat and boots back on and, with tears still running down my face, made my way back outside, walked it off, and got back in the game. I believe we played for another few hours until I came back in. Nothing else was said about it when I came back in. Nothing needed to be said.

Lesson Learned

Some of you may be thinking, "I can't believe this! That's no way to treat a kid, especially one who was hurt. I can't believe he forced you to go back and play hurt when you were at such a young age. You should have stayed in and put ice on it to keep the swelling down." This is very common thinking and why most our kids end up spoiled, gutless, and messed up. This was not about my ankle. Yes, I should have gotten off it. Yes, there should have been ice on it. Yes, it should have been elevated. But what would this really have taught me? If would have taught me to quit when things got tough. It would have taught me to stop when something hurt. It would have taught me to run home every time something happened. It would have taught me to give in to the pain. But what that treatment did, in fact, teach me was to go back, walk it off, and *get back in the game*. In other words, it taught me perseverance.

There are many components to persistence in pursuit of success. There is much more to it then sticking around and trying over and over. That's easy for anyone to do. There are many things along the way that will make you want to quit, force you to quit, cause you pain, set you back, and make your life a living hell. Being persistent in achieving your goals means overcoming all the obstacles you run into along the way. Trust me when I tell you that all the pain and hell you have to go through is always worth it in the end. Just make sure you're suffering for what you really want and believe in.

Quitting

I still believe that quitting is a bad thing and that you should always finish what you set out to do. I am very hardheaded about this one. I also do realize that many athletes may not have the genetics and skills to make it in their sport of choice. I don't think genetics matter in sports. I know there are many coaches freaking out right now. Yes, genetics do matter, and there are many professional athletes that have succeeded with very little work. I know you can't make a jackass a racehorse, but don't tell that to the jackass that's a racehorse in its mind. Here's my point: Most athletes will never make it to the professional level, so the most important thing is to have a good time. This is really why we get involved in sports in the first place. If you're an athlete not suited for a specific sport but who still loves the game, then by all means—stick it out and give it your best shot. The road will be much harder, but we've all seen examples of athletes not suited for a specific sport who nevertheless make it to the top through hard work and determination.

Fishing with Dad

I remember fishing with my dad as a kid. My father had a passion for fishing, hunting, and golf. These were all too relaxed for me. I would rather have run the golf course, swam in the lake, and chopped down trees in the woods. I do not have the composure for leisurely sports. While out on the lake, I would get bored out of my mind. I did like it when I got a fish on the line because that's where the action started. It would last for five minutes and then we would wait what seemed like forever for it to happen again. I remember many trips where we would be on the lake for what seemed like hours and I was ready to quit for the day. I may have tossed the line a hundred times and not gotten one bite. Over and over I would have no luck or any indication that fish were even in the lake at all. But I knew that, if I quit for the day, I had a 100% chance of not catching anything. But, if I tossed my line out one more time, then my chances would go up—and then I would get a strike, just after I was about ready to quit. If I'd known there would be a fish with my next catch, I would never have thought of quitting. If I'd known that even on cast No. 102 I'd get a fish, I would never have thought of quitting. You know what? Life doesn't work that way. If it did, everyone would have fish on the line. You may have success with your first cast, or your fiftieth. You never know unless you toss the line out.

Here's a poem I've carried in my wallet since I was 12 years old. It's my daily reminder to never quit when things get tough. I can't count the number of times I've pulled this out when I was ready to give up. It helped me totally change my focus from feeling sorry for myself to "getting back in the game":

DON'T QUIT!

When things go wrong as they sometimes will
When the road you're trudging seems all uphill
When the funds are low and the debts are high
And you want to smile, but you have to sigh
When care is pressing you down a bit
Rest, if you must, but don't you quit.

Life is queer, with its twists and turns
As everyone of us sometimes learns
And many a failure turns about
When he/she might have won had he/she stuck it out
Don't give up though the pace seems slow
You may succeed with another blow.

Success is failure turned inside out
The silver tint of the clouds of doubt
And you never can tell how close you are
It may be near when it seems so far
So stick to the fight when you're hardest hit
It's when things seem worst that you must not quit.

Author unknown

Chapter Ten

Flexibility

A large portion of success is derived from flexibility.
It is all very well to have principles,
rules of behavior concerning right and wrong.
But it is quite as essential to know when to
forget as when to use them.

Alice Foote MacDougall

To change and to change for the
better are two different things.

German proverb

Only the wisest and stupidest
of men never change.

Confucius

It is not necessary to change.
Survival is not mandatory.

W. Edwards Deming

If we don't change, we don't grow.
If we don't grow, we aren't really living.

Gail Sheehy

He that will not apply new remedies must expect
new evils; for time is the greatest innovator.

Francis Bacon

Life belongs to the living,
and he who lives must be prepared for changes.

Johann Wolfgang von Goethe

The only man who behaved sensibly was my tailor;
he took my measurement anew every time he saw me,
while all the rest went on with their old
measurements and expected them to fit me.

George Bernard Shaw

It's the most unhappy people
who most fear change.

Mignon McLaughlin

Just because everything is different
doesn't mean anything has changed.

Irene Peter

Flexible (as defined by the American Heritage Dictionary):
1. Capable of being bent or flexed; pliable.
2. Capable of being bent repeatedly without injury or damage.
3. Susceptible to influence or persuasion; tractable.
4. Responsive to change; adaptable: *a flexible schedule.*

Change

The biggest lesson I have learned "under the bar" is in dealing with change and being flexible. The development of physical strength is a very tricky thing. What worked for you at the last meet may not work for you at this meet. What worked last year no longer works this year. All you thought you knew about training is constantly challenged by new research. Different methods you have never heard of are producing unreal results with other lifters. Your body is not the same as it was five years ago. The bottom line: All the variables are changing. As a lifter you have to be willing to embrace change and become more flexible in your approach to your goals. Is this any different with any other life goal?

Comfort Zone

I used to be as hardheaded as they come with my own training methods. I had a plan that was working and continued to work for many years. Then my luck ran out and my plan quit working. I looked at other methods but was unwilling to change to anything that was outside my comfort zone. We all get caught up in our own comfort zones. We're happy there. We don't have to think that much. It requires zero risk. It's what we know best. But it's also the greatest cause of stress when things don't go well. We can't figure out why and are too scared and hardheaded to break out of the zone to see what else the world has to offer. This will continue until one of two things happen: We either quit on the goal or we become so frustrated and discouraged that, finally, the pain of staying where we are becomes worse than the fear of trying something new. More often than not, the change brings us much closer to our goals—many times exceeding them.

The Map

After becoming discouraged and suffering a major injury, I did make a change to my training program—and this change was *huge*. Think of it this way: I had a map of the way things were to be done. Within this map I had every variable I felt important to the training process, from the number of sets to rest and recovery. The change I had to make did not mean changing a few of the variables of the plan. I could not stick with *some* of what I felt had worked. Instead, I had to change the entire *map*. We've all developed our own maps over the years. These maps help us find the way to our goals. But there are problems with maps: They are very hard to keep current, you always run into detours, there are roads you suddenly can't find—the list goes on and on. The point is, eventually, we all get lost, forget where we are, run into dead ends, and lose our way. This is when we should stop and ask for directions. Yet we continue driving around getting more and more frustrated by the minute. I was so frustrated with my lack of progress that I needed to toss the entire map and go get a new one and start from scratch. My goal never changed, but my path to it was not working and had to change. Changing the map was not easy and required more from my belief system than I would have liked. The new map, however, has taken me to cities I never knew existed, far exceeding any strength training goals I used to have. Are you using the right map?

Is It Working?

I have conducted hundreds of strength and conditioning seminars throughout the past several years. The one thing I always find the most common is the unwillingness of many of the coaches to change. This blows my mind—why did they spend the money on the seminar in the first place if they're unwilling to learn and grow? Look, I understand I may not always be right, and there may be many coaches, lifters, trainers, and athletes that do not see training the same way I do (even though more of them should). But they come to my seminars anyway, only to debate and think to themselves, "This won't work for me." How do they know? What they need to be asking is, "Is our current program getting the job done?" Just as *you* should be asking, "Is my current program moving me toward or away from my goals?" Let's face it: If the old game plan—the old map—was working in the first place, would they be at a seminar to learn new methods from me? If you were happily on the way to your goals, would you be reading this book? The most important question you will ever have to ask in your life is, "Is this really working for me?" How you answer it is even more important. You should take the time and really think about it. If you are blasting away and moving forward as you like, then congratulations—you're on the right path. Unfortunately for most of us, this is not the case, and we have to look around to see what else could help us advance. So once again ask yourself, "Is this working?"

Training Paradigms

Why the resistance to change? I have given much thought to this, and it always comes back to a point Steven Covey makes in his book *The Seven Habits of Highly Effective People*. We all create our own paradigms of how the world operates. This becomes the way we see things. Coaches, trainers, and athletes create training paradigms based on past successes, failures, and beliefs. My training paradigm for years was based on what is known as the Western method of periodization. Many of the coaches who I've spoken with over the years also have their own ways of seeing the training process, which they've developed over years. This system may have been what they used when they were still athletes. However, for many of them, the system may not be working as well as it used to, or may have ceased to work at all. Instead of looking at other ways, they continue to stick with the old system for several reasons. First, they truly believe it will work again and they place the blame on the athletes or other factors. Second, they feel they do not have the time to revamp the system they're using. Third, they are too damn lazy. Yes, too lazy. I know I was. It takes time to research all the new material out there. Then once you do, you have to find a way to implement and test it with your current group of athletes. When all you know is what you've done in the past, change becomes a very difficult thing, because you may have to let go of many of your old beliefs to move ahead. You will have to break free from your old paradigms. Are you willing to do so? It is not about who is right and who is wrong. It is about what works best and what will help you reach your goals.

Clarity of Goal

You must become very clear on what your goal really is. For the strength coach, is it to have the best program or to make better athletes? If you're a powerlifter, is it the program you use or getting a bigger squat, bench press, deadlift, and total? Once you're clear on the final outcome you're striving for, then it doesn't matter how you get there, only that you're progressing in the right direction. For example, I know of several lifters who have struggled to try and increase a certain lift for many years. Maybe this is a 700-pound squat or 400-pound bench press. They have been on a specific program for many years that always included the same exercises, sets, reps, etc. They love the way they train so much that they would rather not make progress than try something different. If they get very clear on what they want to achieve (a 700-pound squat or 400-pound bench press), then the method becomes only a means to the goal. The goal must always be very clear for success to happen. How clear are your goals?

New Realities

The reality is that the world is always changing. New technologies are being developed every day. New ideas and methods are being tested every day. What worked very well three years ago is now a thing of the past. We all need to stay ahead of the curve and keep up to date with all the changes that can help us achieve our goals in a faster, more efficient manner. Regardless of how wedded you are to a certain way of doing things, there is a better, faster, more efficient way of doing them out there. If you really think back to your past successes, you will find it was something new, some new idea, that helped you move forward. There was a time when you were stumped and had to find a way around the problem. You took the time to find the best solution and were right back on your way. If the first solution did not work, you found a second, third, fourth, or twentieth one. One way or another you found your way around the problem, and I'm willing to bet it was by using a new idea. We can't forget this process and become content with our old ways. If we do, we'll all get left in the dust, as our competition will blow right past us. Are you stuck in your old ways?

Audible Ready

There is a concept described in *The Little Book of Coaching* by Don Shula and Ken Blanchard: knowing when to change. To quote the authors:

"Many people are struggling right now because they haven't learned the power of flexibility. They are still living in the past. They are scared to move forward. You know why? Because they do not have the confidence to do so. They are afraid of failure. They are fearful of looking stupid. They doubt themselves. They are stuck in a rut."

"Prepare well with a plan—then expect the unexpected and be ready to change that plan."

Training Plans

Many times I've been asked, "Can you write a training program for me?" Nothing irritates me more than this question. They (coaches, athletes, and trainers) assume that this is a very easy process that will take a few minutes to put together. In reality it would take hours to compile all the necessary information and many more to put it together. When it's finally complete, the chance of it working for the athlete is less than 20%. You may be saying to yourself, "Wow, you must really suck at writing programs." You know what? You are 100% correct. A program alone will not yield results. It's the modifications that are made along the way that lead to the success of the program. Let me explain . . .

Coach and Billy

Let's say Billy contacts a coach to write a strength-training program for football. After spending time analyzing Billy, the coach discovers that Billy needs to develop the following skills:

1. Explosiveness
2. Mobility
3. Flexibility
4. General conditioning
5. Triceps strength

6. Correct shoulder balance

7. Exercise technique

8. General football skills

9. VO2 max

Crystal Ball

Next, the coach needs to rank the list in order of importance and come up with a general plan to attack the highest-priority items first. Here comes the first problem. Many of the listed items are dependent upon each other, so listing importance can be a bit of a challenge. Then the coach has to select the best training protocol to use for Billy. This brings in problem No. 2. There are hundreds of protocols to choose from that could help Billy with his goals. So the coach has to select the best exercises for Billy that will address his goals. Now we are at problem No. 3: There are thousands of movements that could help Billy with his weaknesses. Sorry—I forgot one major component. The coach has to have the ability to predict the future. Since he is only writing the program and will not be part of the day-to-day implementation of the plan, the coach needs to have a top-notch, high-tech crystal ball so he can predict how each stimulus will effect Billy. Now there are many coaches and trainers out there who will proclaim they have this ability and that their programs will work for anyone. I am here to tell you *they are dead wrong*! It is just not possible for one to see into the future.

Absolute Best You Can Be

Training is a process that has to be taken day to day. Yes, you need to have a basic plan to work from, but there are so many variables that can change at different rates that you must be willing to adapt your plan accordingly. Let's go back to the example with Billy. One of his weak points is mobility. This is an ability that could be corrected with one exercise or it may take 15 movements. This could be corrected in as little as one week or may take months. All goals have the same factors associated with them. The only way for a strength program to be truly effective is to track the key indicators on a daily or weekly basis. They must always be under observation to make sure they're being adjusted while the rest of the program moves forward. A general program may work and produce general results, but we're all after more than just general results—we're after being the absolute best we can be. Other training variables that also need to be taken into account are associated with the individual training session. Let's say Billy was to begin his program with squats and then move on to hamstring work, abdominal work, and conditioning work. What if the squat took more out of him than expected, and this was all his body could handle for the day? If he still pushed it hard on all the other work, he could send his body into an overtraining state. What if he were to do 315 pounds for five sets of five reps in the squat, but after the first set he knew he would not be able to make five reps on the next set? All these factors need to be addressed as the training session progresses in order to achieve the best results.

Your Plan

So, as you can see, a prescribed training plan is a good idea, but is only that—an idea. The rest has to be pieced together as the session and workouts progress. This is the same with any goal you go after. Your plan will not always work. They seldom ever do. You will have to make many changes to your plan along the way. You should do your best to expect the unexpected and remain flexible, which means always having a back-up. So how flexible are you?

Chapter Eleven

Execution

. . . .

The test of any man lies in action.
Pindar

Let him who would move the world,
first move himself.
Socrates

Not the cry, but the flight of the wild duck,
leads the flock to fly and follow.
Chinese proverb

You can't build a reputation on what
you are going to do.
Henry Ford

A journey of one thousand miles
begins with a single step.
Confucius

He who begins many things
finishes but a few.

Italian proverb

If a man does only what is required of him,
he is a slave. If a man does more
than is required of him,
he is a free man.

Chinese proverb

Confidence is contagious.
So is lack of confidence.

Vince Lombardi

Things come to those who wait.
But only things left by those who hustle.

Abraham Lincoln

Noise proves nothing.
Often a hen who has merely laid an egg
cackles as if she has laid an asteroid.

Mark Twain

Execution (as defined by the American Heritage Dictionary):
1.   The act of executing something.
2.   The manner, style, or result of performance.

Fish

ONE, TWO, THREE, SLAP! I still remember the words and sound of the referee slapping his hand on the mat as I was pinned. How could I forget? I heard the same thing in every match I wrestled during the 1980 and 1981 seasons. When you get pinned as much as I did, you become known as a fish. I was in the seventh and eighth grades these years and was new to the sport. I decided to go out for the wrestling team because I didn't like basketball and wanted to try something different. I loved everything about wrestling—I just wasn't very good at it. Yet this didn't make that much difference to me because, up to that point in my life, I wasn't very good at any sport I participated in.

Back on the Bench

I was excited for the 1982 season because I was going to be one of the oldest on the team. Our junior-high years consisted of seventh, eighth, and ninth grades. I was going to be in the ninth grade and figured that my age and experience should win me a few matches. During conditioning for that season, one of the other team members informed me he would be moving up a weight class and I would have to wrestle off against him each match. He was a much better wrestler than I was, so I began to wonder if I would see any time on the mat at all. I was crushed. Now I would have to sit the bench and watch others help the team.

I had received a weight set for Christmas the year before and had been training three days a week for the past six months. I felt stronger but still knew my teammate would be better based on his record the year before. We still had three or four more weeks of conditioning until we hit the mat for practice.

Waiting for Mom

After each practice, I would wait around for my mom to pick us up. Most of the time, I would just sit on the stairs of the gym and joke around with the other wrestlers on the team. One day, I decided to do something different: I spent the time running the stairs. There may have been two short flights of 15 stairs each. This really didn't matter because I just went up and down and figured I would run five sets and then stop. To this day, I still don't know why I decided to do this. Maybe it was the discipline I had developed from weight training the previous six months. Regardless, I ran. I ran until everyone else was picked up and the gym lights were shut down. As it turned out, my mom was running a little late, so I decided to keep running until she came. After 15 or so laps, I reached the top of the stairs to see Coach Mullen staring down at me.

Coach William Mullen

Coach Mullen is one of my favorite coaches of all time. He sported a full beard and liked to get down on the mat and teach us personally how to get the job done. He also loved to bust our ass with conditioning drills and working most practices on the basics. He was a great motivator who always kept the team fired up to work hard. I still think back to those practices where I could barely walk out of the gym. Coach Mullen had a passion for making winners out of all of us, and I was about to discover firsthand the difference two simple sentences can make in a kid's life.

What Are You Doing?

As he stared down at me, Coach asked, "What are you doing?" I replied that I was sick of getting beat all the time and wanted to win the district tournament at the end of the season. This was a pretty bold statement coming from a kid who had won only one match in the past two years. I'm not sure why I said it. Maybe it was to impress the coach; maybe I said it to make myself feel better. Either way, I said it and the damage was done. What would he say to me? Why did I have to open my mouth? After what seemed to be 10 minutes, but in reality was only a couple of seconds, Coach Mullen took a serious look at me and said, "If you work hard enough, you can do whatever you want to. If you believe you can do it, then I believe you can do it." He then walked down the stairs and into the locker room without a single glance back.

This is all it took. I was just about ready to quit running the stairs when I ran into Coach Mullen. My legs were tired and I was completely worn out from practice. I still remember how bad my feet hurt from all the pounding. Instead, after Coach walked into the locker room, I picked up the pace. I began taking two steps at a time instead of one. My breathing got deeper and deeper, but it didn't faze me a bit. If all I had to do was work hard, then I was going to bust my ass. For the next 45 minutes, I ran the stairs. I don't think it would have mattered if I had to wait another 45 minutes for my mom—I would have run all night! I now had something in my blood that had been missing up to that point. I had been given one of the greatest gifts in life: I now had CON-FIDENCE running through my veins.

This passion continued throughout the rest of the season. I ran the stairs every night after practice. I lifted weights when I got home. On the days we didn't have practice, I went to the local

YMCA and worked on my drop step, escape, and other basic skills for hours on end. I spent my weekends back at the YMCA running, lifting, swimming, and working skills. I would spend the entire day there training. (It took me many years to learn what overtraining was.) I got stronger, faster, and better conditioned then anyone else on the team. Getting through wrestle-offs was not a problem. The wrestler I was afraid would beat me didn't make it past the first period. I finished the year undefeated and went on to win the district tournament with four pins—not one went past 30 seconds into the first period.

I'm not telling you this story to impress you. I was in the ninth grade at the time, hardly an Olympic hopeful. I'm telling you this to impress upon you the power that confidence can have in your life. I'm also telling you this to show you the power one man or woman can have on another life with two simple sentences. I honestly don't know where I'd be today if I hadn't heard those two sentences. That year I learned that if I worked hard and believed in myself, I could accomplish anything. Yes, I knew this before. We all learn this growing up. Our parents tell it to us, we see movies about it, we read about it. But being inspired to *live it* is something completely different. I could have agreed with Coach but stopped running the stairs, not trained any harder, not spent the extra hours working skills—and still had the same piss-poor season. You can *believe* something all you want. You can set all the goals you want. But if you're not willing to pay the price for those goals, then you'll stay exactly where you are.

Execution

The real world is about execution. It's not a matter of who has the best training plan or who has the best idea. The winner is always the one who puts the plan to use and gets the job done.

I've seen lifter after lifter spend countless hours constructing the perfect training and nutrition cycle but never put it to use because, supposedly, it was never good enough. I've also seen lifters train solely on the basis of how they feel when they get into the gym, using no structured training plan, yet they enjoy great success. The difference is in the action. So what is the secret to execution? How do we get the job done? I've heard these questions many times and the answer is always the same: Get off your butt and get to work. Execution is about getting things done. This doesn't mean starting one thing, then another, then a few more. It means getting things finished! Anyone can start a project, but very few carry something out until completion.

Finish what you begin or don't start in the first place! This is where most people make their biggest mistake. They come up with what they think is a great idea and begin putting it to use before they've thought it out. Then halfway through, they decide it may not be the best plan for them. This is a waste of time and could have been avoided with more detailed thought before the project was started. Not every idea you have or every idea someone tells you will work for you. You have to take it in and think about how it can be used or modified to fit your overall needs. If you do decide it's worthwhile, *then* take immediate action: Establish a plan and follow it through to completion.

Excuses

If I had a dollar for every excuse I've heard for lack of progress, I would be a very rich man. "My bench press won't go up," "I can't make first-string on my high school football team," "I don't have enough money," "I don't have time to better educate myself"—the list goes on and on. The bottom line? Who cares?! I don't care and neither does anyone else. The only one who seems to care is the one who's making the excuses.

I say "seems" to care because it's my opinion that they really don't care; if they did, they would do something to try and change the situation.

This is really very simple. If you want success in what you're doing, you're going to have to do the work. It's not enough to *start* the work—you have to do what's necessary to *complete* the work. No one cares about all the things you *tried* to do; they only care about what you've, in fact, done. What was the last thing you finished?

Chapter Twelve

Responsibility

*Choice of attention—to pay attention to this
and ignore that—is to the inner life what choice
of action is to the outer. In both cases, a man is
responsible for his choice and must accept the
consequences, whatever they may be.*

W. H. Auden

*The great thought, the great concern,
the great anxiety of men is to restrict, as much as
possible, the limits of their own responsibility.*

Giosué Borsi

*To what extent is any given man morally responsible
for any given act? We do not know.*

Alexis Carrel

*I am only one; but still I am one.
I cannot do everything, but still I can do something;
I will not refuse to do something I can do.*

Helen Keller

125

Success on any major scale requires you to accept responsibility...in the final analysis, the one quality that all successful people have...is the ability to take on responsibility.

Michael Korda

The reason people blame things on the previous generations is that there's only one other choice.

Doug Larson

You cannot escape the responsibility of tomorrow by evading it today.

Abraham Lincoln

I was taught very early that I would have to depend entirely upon myself; that my future lay in my own hands.

Darius Ogden Mills

As human beings, we are endowed with freedom of choice, and we cannot shuffle off our responsibility upon the shoulders of God or nature. We must shoulder it ourselves. It is our responsibility.

Arnold J. Toynbee

Few things can help an individual more than to place responsibility on him, and to let him know that you trust him.

Booker T. Washington

Responsibility (as defined by the American Heritage Dictionary):
1. The state, quality, or fact of being responsible.

Excuses

Here is a great list of excuses I have collected over the years, told to me by lifters who've had trouble with their training programs and/or missed a maximum attempt:

1. My gym owners do not allow chalk.
2. My gym does not have the equipment I need.
3. I do not have time to do extra workouts.
4. It is hard for me to make it to the gym four times per week.
5. It is hard for me to get away from work to go to a meet.
6. My powerlifting gear does not fit right.
7. The bar fell out of the groove on that last lift.
8. I used to be able to do that for three reps.
9. I had to use a crappy bar.
10. I did not have good spotters.
11. The rack was too narrow.
12. The J hooks in the rack were set too low.
13. I did not get enough rest between sets.
14. I felt rushed.
15. My wraps were too tight.
16. The meet started too late.
17. The meet ran too long.

18. The meet ran too fast.
19. The flight drained me.
20. My gear did not get to the meet.
21. My partners were not motivating me.
22. There were too many good-looking girls in the gym at the time.
23. The weights were not "official."
24. The bench was too high.
25. The bench was too low.
26. The bar did not have a good grip to it.
27. The bar was too sharp.
28. My suit was too tight.
29. My bench shirt was too tight.
30. My briefs were too tight.
31. My shirt was too big.
32. My suit was too big.
33. I did not have my ammonia caps.
34. I did not have lunch.
35. I ate like crap all weekend.
36. I did not sleep at all last night.
37. I do not have enough money.
38. My spouse does not like me training.
39. My car broke down.
40. I was sick.
41. The rain made my joint feels tight.
42. My shoulder hurt (or any other body part).

43. I forgot my liniment.

44. My training did not go well.

45. My coach had me go up to a weight that was too heavy.

46. My coach did not write a good program.

47. I forgot my sports drink.

48. My supplements did not work.

49. My triceps strength never came around.

50. My body weight was off.

The Common Denominator

Here is the best part. I have also used every one of these excuses—plus hundreds of others. That was before I discovered the real secret to making strength gains. Reread the list again and see if you can find anything common to all of them. Take your time if you have to. Have you found it yet? Try again and look deeper. Read between the lines and go deeper than the surface. Find it yet? Let me help you: If *I've* used every one of them, then the common factor is *me*. The person who makes the list of excuses is always the common denominator. The responsibility always falls back on the one who makes the excuses.

Let's review a few of the items on the list to better illustrate the point. We will start with No. 45: "My coach had me go up to a weight that was too heavy." I can see how you might feel this was the coach's fault—but who decided he would be your coach? Did you lift up to your potential? Could you have told him it was too much? Now let look at No. 39: "My car broke down." Who bought the car? Do you get it checked on a regular basis? Could you have called someone to pick you up?

A training partner of mine got into a car accident two weeks before a meet and ended up rolling the car in a ditch. He made it to the gym because he asked the officer to drop him off. He did this so he would not miss a training session and could continue training for the meet. Let's try one more. How about No. 2: "My gym does not have the equipment I need." Did you join the gym? Have you asked for the equipment you need? As you can see, the blame will always come back to you. You may be thinking this is not always true; there are always some things that are beyond your control. I agree—crappy things can and do happen. That's life, and what keeps life exciting. It's not the crappy things in themselves that break us down, but how we feel and react to those things. If you spend your time and energy trying to place blame and complain, then you're not using that time trying to find a solution. The minute you shut up and begin to take responsibility, you will begin to find a solution. Even if you feel it's not your fault, *take responsibility and get over it*. The alternative will only result in more blaming, conflict, and disruption in your life. None of these things will bring you closer to success.

The Competitive-Squat Process

The competitive squat is the best example of taking responsibility I can think of. You begin training for a meet many weeks or months beforehand. You may or may not have someone help you with your training. You're required to make it to the gym and perform the training sessions that will prepare you for your next squat goal. You rearrange your life to make sure you make it to the gym. Throughout the weeks of training, you make the proper training decisions to help you peak for the lift. When you get to the meet you'll have a few helpers who'll help you get into your squat gear, wrap your knees, and get to the platform. Up to this point you've had the help of training partners, coaches, helpers, family, and many others. When you get under the bar and take the weight off the rack, guess what? *You're on your own.* At this point, nobody else can lift the weight for you. This is your moment of truth, and you know it. If you fail, then it's your responsibility to fix it. Life is much the same way. There will be others who'll be with you and help guide you along the path. But there will be a time when you'll be on your own. However, to ensure success, you always want to surround yourself with others who will bring out the best in you. If you surround yourself with people who bring you down, then you have only yourself to blame.

Decisions: You Must First Decide

You have to look at the decisions you make and how they affect the lifestyle you would like to lead. Are these decisions consistent with the life you want, or are they working against you? You see, for every effect in your life there is a cause. If things are not going the way you like, then you have to look back and try to find the cause. With the above example of the competitive squat, if the lifter was not successful, then there is a cause for this effect. The key to success is finding this cause, taking responsibility for it, and then fixing it so it will not happen again. If the lifter was successful, then the same holds true. He needs to look back and find the cause for the success and make sure to keep it as part of his program. You may find that there's more than one cause for your failure. This is usually the case. So determine what all the causes are and fix each one of them, one by one, until the problems and obstacles are gone. This may sound too simple, but that's because the solutions to many problems usually are. The hard part is deciding if you want to take the needed responsibility to fix it. This is why 90% of the people in this world would rather blame someone else for their problems. Your first line of action is to decide that you will eliminate those things that are keeping you from what you really want. Only you can do this. You are the only one that has control over what you think, what you read, with whom you associate, what you listen to, and the words that will come out of your mouth. These things are your responsibility. So, in the end, your success or failure depends on YOU.

Responsibility is a difficult subject to write about because its simplicity causes many people to underestimate it or miss it altogether. It is so much easier to push the responsibility onto other people. Just look around us—you see it everywhere. Gossip is going on in every house, gym, and business around the world. We're all so wrapped up in what other people are or are not doing, when we should be worry about getting off our own asses and doing what we need to do for ourselves. We blame teachers for our messed-up kids, when it's parents who sit them in front of the TV for hours on end with little social interaction. We blame the food we eat for obesity in our society, when we all know the food does not jump down our throat by itself. We blame the government for all that is wrong with the world today, but sit back in our recliners and say, "I don't have the time to help anybody else." We blame our bosses for being too tough, but then spend the majority of our time working on low-priority items. We bitch about not having enough money, but never try to find a way to make more. We get discouraged when someone is stronger than us, but don't try to find out what they did to get that way. If you turn on the TV, all you see are people placing the blame for their problems on their parents, spouses, girlfriends, boyfriends, kids—you name it. When given the chance, they always blame someone else. This seems to be the new "American Way," and it makes me want to puke!

No Free Lunch

Look, bad things happen—that's life. I've had many bad things happen to me, and I'm sure you have, too. It's what we do about them that make the difference. We have two choices: We can place the blame on someone else, or we can get on with our life and learn from our problems and tragedies. I remember when I was in college, I was speaking to my mom on the phone. I had run out of money, had no food in the kitchen, and had not eaten since early that morning. "What happened to the money you had?" my mom asked. I told her I had spent it. I was then told, "Well, I guess this is a learning experience." Learning experience! I was starving—screw the learning experience! I needed food! You know what? I didn't get the money. Instead, I found some food, got a part-time job, and learned to better manage my money. Was I pissed? Yes, I was pissed, but I got over it and became grateful for the help I did get. There are many others a hell of a lot worse off than me. I could have placed the blame on my mother for letting me "starve," but would that have put food in my stomach? This was not about eating or not eating—it was about becoming more responsible. Now that I'm a parent, I know it would have been much easier for her to give me the money than it was to teach me this lesson. But being a parent also means being responsible for raising your children to be successful in this world. What is more important, one meal or a lifetime of success?

Loading the Bar

It is funny how everything you really need to know is right there in front of your face. I see this with power lifters, strength coaches, personal trainers, friends, family and everyone else I speak to. This book has not been about training, but it is. This book was not written about business, but it was. This book was not compiled to help you better your relationships, but it could be. This book was not written as a road map to help you achieve your goals, but it ended up that way. You see this book was written to show you that all the lessons I needed to reach my personal, financial and business goals were with me all the time. It just took 25 years to figure it out. Let me explain.

Training for the Meet

When I first started power lifting I decided that I wanted to compete with the best (Aim). The first thing I found were other power lifters who could help me out (Teamwork) and set a schedule that would allow me to train with them. I also bought every book I could find on power lifting, bodybuilding and strength training (Education). It did not take long before I realized that I had to be at every training session if I wanted to get better (Dedication) and that I had to have a plan designed around developing the strength I need in the squat, bench press and dead lift. More importantly I had to find a way to make the plan work (Execution). For the most part, the training plan worked but there were many times I had to come up with a different plan after suffering some type of set back (Flexibility). Many of these set backs were the result of trying new things, over training or time management issues. These set backs (Risks) had to be worked into the plan if I wanted to move forward in the sport.

Early on I discovered that you can lie to others about what you can lift but you can't lie to yourself. You can either lift the weight or you can't. There are no other options, so it is best to be truthful with yourself and others (Honesty). There is only one way you can lift big weights and you have to have the right mindset to do it (Attitude). If you do not have the right attitude, no matter what endeavor you pursue, you will not be successful. Your attitude has to stay positive but open. If you are not open to coaching from others (Criticism) then you will only go so far. The advice you receive is a special gift that needs to be harnessed. Even if the gift is harsh there is always a lesson to be learned. I had to learn that it did not matter who the advice came from, only that it keeps coming.

I have spent over 20 years in a sport and many times it has taken over 5 years to reach a new personal record (Perseverance). It may have taken 5 years to reach the goal but strength is not a linear process. You do not get 5 lbs stronger every couple months. This may work for beginners but you soon realize that those 5 pounds are not as easy as they used to be. You also find that when you do break through it is usually not 5 pounds; it is more like 40 – 50 pounds. Many will credit this 50 pound increase because of a new program or a new movement. While this is true they fail to mention that it took 5 years to find what they needed. During this time, they continued to work on the base structure and developed a better foundation to work from. This is not an easy process and requires that you learn to take personal responsibility (Responsibility) for your training. Regardless of what you think, or anyone else thinks it always comes back on you.

What Is in Your Past?

We all have meets in our past. I have never met a person who has not been successful at least one time in their life. If you go back and look very closely at what enabled your success you will see these values will be there. The key is to realize that they were there, you lived by them and they work. Then you need to apply these same values to other areas of your life. Most people do not take the time to think about how simple it really is. They want some special 8-step process that will guarantee success. They want to be told what to do. I was the same way. I discovered that I always knew what I needed to do to be successful. I just never put all the steps together.

This is your wake up call to put the steps together and be successful. You have always known what you need to do. Now do it!

About Dave Tate

Dave Tate has been a competitive Power Lifter since 1984 and has achieved personal best lifts of 935lbs in the Squat, 610lbs in the Bench Press and 740lbs in the deadlift. He is the founder and president of Elite Fitness Systems (EliteFTS.com) and is a renowned speaker on the development  opment of maximal strength and development. Dave has also authored hundreds of strength and conditioning articles and is on the advisory board for Men's Fitness and Sly magazine.

Other Products by Dave Tate and EliteFTS

- The Westside Seminar Video

- The Dynamic Squat Manual

- The Dynamic Bench Manual

- The Training Templates Manual

- The Band Manual

- The Lower Body Exercise Index DVD

- The Upper Body Exercise Index DVD

Plus thousands of articles and Q and A's

www.EliteFTS.com